ON MUSIC AND MUSICIANS

MANUEL DE FALLA

ON MUSIC
AND MUSICIANS

WITH AN
INTRODUCTION AND NOTES BY
FEDERICO SOPEÑA

———

TRANSLATED BY
DAVID URMAN
AND
J. M. THOMSON

MARION BOYARS · LONDON · BOSTON

Published simultaneously
in Great Britain and in the United States in 1979 by
Marion Boyars Ltd
18 Brewer Street, London WIR 4AS
and
Marion Boyars Inc.
99 Main Street, Salem. New Hampshire 03079

Originally Published in Spain in 1950 by
Espasa-Calpe, S.A., Madrid
under the title *Escritos sobre Música y Músicos*

Australian distribution by Thomas C. Lothian
4-12 Tattersalls Lane, Melbourne, Victoria 3000

Canadian distribution by Burns & MacEachern Ltd.
Suite 3, 62 Railside Road, Don Mills, Ontario

© 1950, 1972 Herederos de Manuel de Falla
© This Translation Marion Boyars Publishers, 1979

ISBN 0 7145 2600 2 cased edition

Filmset in Monophoto Imprint 101
by A. Brown & Sons Ltd., Hull, England

CONTENTS

Introduction by Federico Sopeña   vii
Translators' Preface   xiii

I   Back from Paris   1
    Enrique Granados, an evocation of his work   7
    Igor Stravinsky: The great musician of our time   9
    Introduction to the new music   13
    Contemporary French music   22
    Preface to the *Enciclopedia Abreviada de Música* by
    Joaquin Turina   27
    Our Music   30

II   Debussy   37

III   Felipe Pedrell   49

IV   Inquests   67

V   Wagner   77
    Notes on Richard Wagner, on the fiftieth
    anniversary of his death

VI   Ravel   91

APPENDIX   99
    The *Cante jondo*
    I   Analysis of the musical elements of *cante*   101
        jondo
    II   Influence of these songs on modern   106
        European music
    III   The Guitar   110
    The *Cante Jondo Competition*   112

INTRODUCTION

by Federico Sopeña

THE IDEA OF collecting Manuel de Falla's most significant writings was by no means new to me. My first article on a musical theme – a jejune article, almost that of a teenager – was entitled 'Falla leaves us for America', and my first lecture was about his writings. This seemed a novelty to many, and behind that feeling I could sense a sad ignorance. Since then, I have written on several occasions on the essays collected here, in which I have both expressed my admiration and raised some questions. I have never published them, it is true, prefering to keep such commentary for a book I still see as remote: Falla's biography. Remote, because such a book cannot be forced: it requires a certain maturity. Even a month ago I did not see it in this way; my excuse for postponing it was that don Manuel was returning for the première of his *Atlántida*. Now, without the hope of a personal, intimate knowledge of the composer, in this strange and bitter sense of loss, I feel even more strongly the necessity of waiting. Falla's biography is to be observed in the development of his successors, who have already reached their maturity. Above all, one must go through note after note, year after year, landscape after landscape, for as long a time as God permits.

What is urgent, instead, is to find the intermediate steps that might lead to the biography, to get people to break their silence, so as to help us on the journey, to find a way through the empty verbiage and commonplaces uttered on the occasion of the master's death. Adolfo Salazar has promised a biography. Whether the testimony of somebody so close to Falla appears or not, the important thing is to allow our memories to mature, and to gather our recollections. Therefore, I publish here neither letters nor reminiscences, nor even articles or statements don Manuel felt distant from, or dissatisfied with. Instead, I have chosen those writings that, from their subject and their aim, represent months, perhaps years, of continued reflection about his own creation. They are, moreover, the best introduction to his work; and such a title would be the most appropriate and most modest for my tribute.

Before beginning, it is necessary to draw a general picture of Falla as a writer. We know that in his youth he felt a literary vocation, encouraged by Zurbarán, by the sea, and by music itself. His writings show that it was not pure play: Falla was a true writer. He wrote only when it was necessary, but without giving us any painful impressions of a dearth of means, of an awkward slowness, or of slackness. Emilio García Gómez[1], who was an intimate friend of don Manuel, told us about the anguish, the childish concern, the procession of cautious and apprehensive feelings that surrounded a letter or an article. That is why his essays, as his compositions, impress upon us that every word, every expression, has a definite character. Falla was a writer: his essays, as his music, seem to originate in the freest and most radiant spontaneity. His style is so personal, so calm and vital at the same time, that it seems, and it is, some consolation, that we hear his very voice beside us.

The whole of Falla is in his writings – a frequently absorbed, concerned, Falla, but also ironic and cheerful as occasion demanded. Proof of this are those delightful verses I cannot forget, sent by Falla to Turina together with his *Piezas españolas* – 'don Vicente' is, of course, Vincent d'Indy:

> Manuel de Falla, of Cádiz,
> with the highest of respects,
> dedicates this manuscript
> to Turina, the Sevillian.
> You know, my dear Joaquín,
> that these four little pieces
> are only light impressions
> without tail, or head, or end.
> And thus there is not in them
> neither 'de la musique ni plan
> ni même de jolis coins',
> as don Vicente does say.

Since Debussy, there is no composer who has not written what I would call 'manifesto prose'. It is useful to remember this when placing Falla's writings. At the time of his arrival in Paris, composers astringently made known their position as between music and the writings of the Schola and of the Conservatoire. Vincent d'Indy wrote a great deal; above all, a biography of César Franck, in which all the facets of his personality are present: good nature, bad temper, worship of his 'father', Franck, the patriotism of a provincial nobleman, the lack of a sense of irony. Confronting d'Indy are the critical writings of Debussy, and not those of Fauré, the director of the Conservatoire, who wrote little and without taking risks. Debussy's writings, which Falla must have devoured, are deeply – perhaps excessively – concerned with literature. Unlike the titles of his works, they are not *poèmes en prose*, but incisive, ironic pieces, so ironic that, paradoxically, they can become naïve, such as the *Interview with the chevalier Gluck*. Lyrical elements sometimes appear, especially in the shorter articles of the *Revue Blanche,* but only briefly. Debussy always conceals his innermost feelings. He did not write technical essays; in this sense, they are less 'professional' than those of Paul Dukas in the *Revue Hebdomadaire*. Debussy, the innovator, tried to make himself understood by those who so efficaciously backed his cause, the poets and painters. These are essays for an intelligent person to read, without that detail intelligible only to the professional. But they are not purely literary either. The study of the Ninth Symphony, the study on César Franck are meant to express ideas on music, clearly and definitively, they are meant to be symbols of a new epoch.

The French artist, whether painter, musician or dancer, is usually facile with the pen, helped by a stylistic elegance implicit in his culture. Spaniards living in Paris, those who were for a long time the centre of curiosity and of affectionate attention, remained in a Celtiberian silence. Falla found nothing written by Zuloaga or by Albéniz. When they wrote something, they confined themselves to a prudent and non-committed tone; they provided anecdotes, but no essays.

Ricardo Viñes is an important exception, it is true. A Celtiberian, very *fin de siècle* in his poems, he appears as perfectly refined, witty, and bucolic in those short essays about the 'three wizards of wound', written after the rage of the controversy concerning the extreme refinements of Erik Satie and Paul Valéry. After the war there came a deluge of writings and of manifestos about Jean Cocteau's *Le Coq*. The *Revue Musicale*, the 'portraits-dialogues' by Coeurcy, and all the musical sections of newspapers and magazines provide good testimony to its liveliness. The generation of European musicians centred in Paris spread the prose of manifestos: Alfredo Casella is a good example. Alongside it came didactic work, the recension, for the sake of the younger generation at home, of what had been learned in Paris. This was the invaluable service rendered by the *Enciclopedia Abreviada de Música* of Joaquín Turina. On a still more theoretical level, came the works that initiated harmonic révolutions on the basis of a newly-coined nationalism: prefaces to song books, collected personally, in the manner of Béla Bartók.

Stravinsky's writings are decisive for contemporary European music. Stravinsky was not a writer; his *Memoires* were written with the help of Roland Manuel, but they are invaluable documents. As in his music, Stravinsky defended his privacy; he was only interested in telling the genesis of each work, his polemical attitude. In the course of this work we shall come back to Stravinsky's *Memoires*: suffice it to recall now the passion unleashed by the reading of it, a passion expressed in 'definitions' uttered everywhere, in exaggerations, and in panegyrics. These *Memoires*, so bare, so balanced, so partial, with their deep note of final melancholy – the artist who does not resign himself to being a solitary – are like the 'consciousness' of European music.

We now have the framework for Falla's writings. As to their reception in Spain, this was painfully non-existent, apart from the response of Felipe Pedrell, Falla's ideological spur. To the best of my knowledge none of the Spanish writers who did not know Pedrell ever quote Falla's essays.

Since Goya, no Spanish name had been more universally known than that of Falla. Neither *Musicalia,* contemporary of *El Amor Brujo* and of *Noches en los jardines de España,* nor *The Dehumanization of Art* – written when essays about Spanish music were appearing everywhere – took this music into account. I should like to know on how many desks of Spanish writers one would be likely to find *Revue Musicale,* which published the 'confessions' of Barrès, of Gide, of the countess of Noailles, of Claudel, of Valéry, of Marcel . . . This lack of a favourable atmosphere makes Falla's essays more significant. 'There is to them' no attitude of protest like that of Pedrell. Falla defends himself better, with a more elegant style, where Pedrell had cried out bitterly. Today, what was a cry in the wilderness sounds like a 'rediscovery'. By contrast, Debussy's essays were the product of an ambience and of a community; they were born, perhaps, in the very circle of Stéphane Mallarmé.

Falla, modestly, always avoids referring to his own life. In this sense, his writings show a close affinity to those of Stravinsky. But neither in Debussy's nor in Stravinsky's is there as precise an educational concern as in Falla's, who evidently always bears in mind the hypothetical young generations. Falla repudiated the idea of being the head of a school. Like all authentic founders, he only preached freedom, so necessary against the artistic stagnation of Spain. He preached freedom, he took an individual attitude towards romanticism, far more straightforward than that of Stravinsky, the panegyrist of Tchaikovsky. Thus Falla's writings are essays that every Spaniard concerned with the great problems of nationalism and universality should know but does not. I could make an anthology of all the astonished expressions which greeted me since last year, whenever I spoke of collecting these writings.

The *Comisaría General de Música* of the *Ministerio de Educación Nacional* collected these writings of Falla in a limited edition as a tribute, published free of charge. This marked a highpoint of the *Comisaría's* aim of serving Spanish music. Since the first tasks undertaken by this institution, presided over by that constant friend of Manuel de Falla, Joaquín Turina, a noble approval was evident. In the 1941 season we invited his favourite disciple, Ernesto Halffter, to come from Lisbon, and very carefully staged the revival of *El Retablo de maese Pedro,* as part of a series of performances intended as a homage to de Falla. Everybody collaborated in a revival that for many young people was like a premiére.

For this first publication, I received invaluable help in that Germán de Falla put together widely-scattered papers and encouraged me towards perfection in the smallest detail. She thus made it possible. I wish, therefore, to express my deepest gratitude, which is not only that of the writer who acknowledges receiving details important for his work, but, above all, towards those who wrote sensitive long letters with new truths about Falla. I am also grateful to Gerardo Diego for finding the article published in the *Revista Musical.*

I dedicate this edition to Emilio García Gómez, to whom we are indebted for his constant devotion to the master. On the happy occasion of the revival of *El retablo de maese Pedro,* the greatest and most reliable help which came from the literary field was that of this writer friend, a representative of the Falla who lived at Granada. The tribute was also witnessed by Ignacio Zuloaga and Ricardo Viñes, who represented something different: the Paris that made Manuel de Falla almost happy.

Salamanca, Colegio de Santiago.
Festivity of Saint Thomas Aquinas, 1948

[1] Emilio García Gómez, the greatest Spanish Arabist, author of several books on Arabigo-Andalusian literature. (Trans.)

TRANSLATORS' PREFACE

FOR THIS English edition of Falla's writings we have included all the original essays in the Spanish edition of 1948, for the sake of historical completeness, even when on occasion the substance seemed slight or ephemeral. These weaknesses are more than compensated for by the lucidity, charm and texture of Falla's writings, the clear light he throws on to the way Spanish composers gradually refound their place in the western musical tradition. Nobody more than Falla shows what the artistic and personal foundations of this recrudescence had to be.

In trying to find an English prose rhythm to parallel that of Falla, we should like to make the following points. Falla's prose – especially in the essays in the first section – is far removed from that of his contemporaries, the brilliant writers of the generation of Ortega y Gasset or Pío Baroja, to quote only two of the most important names, who restored to Spanish prose the splendid rigour and sobriety it had lost in the general dissolution of values Spain's political twilight caused. Falla's writings could much more easily be stylistically related to those of the early and mid-nineteenth century. A first reading of the Spanish original gives an impression of nervous energy, of restlessness, which the Spanish editor feels may stem from Falla's passionate involvement in his subjects. This permeates the discourse at every level: the construction of sentences, paragraphs, and the articles as a whole.

Within the sentence the most remarkable features are a superabundant and not always enriching use of adjectives, as well as an excessive, because unnecessary, number of words to represent concepts that are not always proportionately complex. Sentences are often too long, and this leads to repetitions intended to clarify the sense of the discourse, which by now has grown somewhat confused. Thus the prose carries a certain heaviness and pomposity which the ideas themselves most certainly lack.

Moreover the composer's ideas do not progress in a straight line from one sentence, or paragraph, to the next. We find repetitious movements back and forth, even between sentences and between paragraphs, even within a sentence. This looseness of style undermines the tremendous interest created by the actual substance of the articles, by the power of Falla's original mind.

This presented a problem and a choice for the translators. We could either have eliminated all awkwardnesses and superimposed a clarity and simplicity of style unlike the creative struggles of the original, or we could have left the material largely as it was. To do this might well have alienated the English reader from penetrating far enough to appreciate the depth and insights of Falla's thoughts. So we have chosen a compromise solution and preserved as much of the original style and flavour as would not impede the flow of the argument. It is impossible to render Falla plain: but also reprehensible to render him coloured. Thereby we hope this collection will add to the stature of a remarkable musician and with this knowledge of the environment in which he worked, make his musical achievements seem all the fresher; products of an intuitive, gifted, sensitive personality.

David Urman
J. M. Thomson
London/Wellington March 1978

Acknowledgment

The translators wish to thank Arthur Searle for his invaluable help in revising the text.

I

BACK FROM PARIS

BACK FROM PARIS

THIS FIRST section of Falla's writings provides an accurate picture of Madrid's musical atmosphere at the time as Falla and Turina arrived from Paris. Their return coincided with the death of Enrique Granados, which, naturally enough, intensified the sense of responsibility in those wanting to be the protagonists of a renewal in Spanish music.

While they were living in Paris, the names of Falla and Turina were always linked, especially in reports of success such as 'Spaniards in Paris'. Until the war their trips home were brief and made with a return ticket mentality. It was not only the European war that accounted for their permanent return. Already masters of a precise technique, they felt it their duty to contribute to the enrichment of Spain's musical life. We see Falla and Turina proselytizing with lectures, piano playing, and singing at Madrid's Ateneo.

It was not without a recondite and painful effort that Falla took up the task of propagandist. When still in Paris he had been dreaming of the *cármenes,* the country houses at Granada, or of retreats at Cordova. He had been dreaming of solitude, which he gave up in his generous eagerness to spur on Spanish musicians. We can follow Falla's sojourn in Madrid by means of a little documentation and much guesswork. At hand we have the periodicals of that time: the premières of *El amor brujo,* the *Canciones,* the *Noches,* had already been given. Success was not enough for one who did not seek it as an end in itself. Falla, though yearning for solitude, considered that his voice had become mature enough to speak to a new generation still to come into being, a generation ready for Europe's contemporary music. The first thing to do; therefore, was to inform, and that was exactly what Falla did.

There is always a danger in a solitary person adopting the admonitory tones of a manifesto. In the following pages we witness a nervous, passionate Falla, writing hastily, sometimes restlessly, and even incorrectly.

All these writings go together with other parallel efforts to orientate Spanish culture towards Europe: the Sociedad Nacional de Música, the first works of Adolfo Salazar, the Orquesta Filarmónica itself, the coming to Spain of Diaghilev's Ballets, the travels of Ricardo Viñes. All this appears to have a certain polemical tone by comparison with another milieu which, paradoxically, could be considered progressive – the Sociedad Filarmónica and the now rather faded debate about Wagner. The explanation is not difficult. Spain had remained outside the trends of European music during the whole of the nineteenth century; now, suddenly, the Sociedad Filarmónica hastened to promote this as the music of the day. Its mentor was Cecilio de Roda. According to him, a Spanish composer should look towards Vienna and Leipzig. Not only the most recent French music by Debussy and Ravel, but also that of Albéniz, bore the brunt of de Roda's criticism. The 'national opera', 'nationalism' itself, had to join in the exasperated neo-classicism of post-Wagnerian Germany. Amongst the Spanish composers, some such as Conrado del Campo preferred the calmer post-romanticism of Strauss, Franck and the fountainheads, Wagner, and Beethoven's last quartets. But the majority gathered around the official doctrine and sheltered under the more trivial formula of romantic formalism. On the other hand, as *Musicalia* attests, Mendelssohn was applauded in the concert hall and Debussy hissed. The Teatro Real did not want to hear of *Pelléas*, and certainly not of *La Vida breve*.

To be able to judge these writings adequately – especially the piece on Stravinsky – we have to imagine what it meant to spend ten years in Paris, in Debussy's Paris, during the most creative, restless and productive years of European contemporary music, to consider oneself a disciple of Debussy, to believe that between the *Iberia* of Debussy and that of Albéniz the decisive chapter of Spanish nationalism was being written. And then, back in Madrid, to witness something much worse than the hissing in the concert hall, the critic's lack of understanding and the stagnation of official teaching. *El amor brujo* was applauded and its worth was assessed by relating it to *Peer Gynt*! What, then, did the critics make of *L'apres-midi*?

This phenomenon happened time and again all over Europe: Bartók had to suffer as much, or more, in Hungary; Casella in Italy. A whole generation prepared to get rid of the picturesque. That is why they had to fight against romantic music, although this fight, as we shall see, would later on become stagnant. The actual enemy was, at bottom, the worst legacy of romanticism; passionate feeling become a formula. These are Falla's fundamental words, though they might have been said by Bartók or by Casella: 'It is my humble opinion that the classical forms of our art should only be studied to learn order, equilibrium and an often exemplary technique. They should stimulate the creation of new forms in which those same qualities appear, never by being copied (unless some other special formula is pursued) like a cooking recipe'. These statements, and similar ones by Stravinsky about neo-classicism and 'revivals', are the clearest programme that has been proposed for European music.

Falla honestly insists on his dissenting views about some of the appraisals in Turina's *Enciclopedia*. The debate over d'Indy and Debussy goes on, but without bitterness or broken friendship, it continues on the 'nationalistic' side. Falla saw Franck and Debussy in a very different way, but he looked at them as a composer; he was perfectly aware that, from a didactic point of view, the *Enciclopedia abreviada de la música* had already gained public recognition. It would be unnecessary to stress here the friendship between Falla and Turina, diverse though their ways might be. At that time Turina was staging, as a director, the first version of *El sombrero de tres picos*...

These ideas appearing in the preface to the *Enciclopedia* had already been unfolded by Falla in previous articles and lectures; the foundations are thereby laid of what will become, a few years later, the splendid essay on Debussy. We can hear the sharp sound of a radical nationalism, quite different from Turina's. It would take a more definite shape when the liberating mission had been fulfilled. The magazine in which this material was published, bravely continued the effort of the *Revista Musical* of Bilbao. We find young Salazar writing there and he it was who drew our attention to three of the articles in this first section.

ENRIQUE GRANADOS
AN EVOCATION OF HIS WORK

'Revista Musical Hispanoamericana', Madrid, April 1916

I START writing in deep emotion after experiencing the music of Enrique Granados, music that so many times conjured up things and beings from times past, and now helps me to evoke the great artist who composed it. Those of us who have had the good fortune to hear him perform his own works will never forget the strong aesthetic impression we experienced.

Therefore now, while playing those of his piano works I most prefer, I unconsciously repeated the rhythmic accents, the nuances, the inflexions which he used to impress on his music. And, in doing so, it seemed to me that the soul of Granados was present in the tremulous sonorities he wrote down for us, as if it were his testament.

I shall never forget his reading of the first part of his opera *Goyescas* which he gave us in Paris, at Joaquín Nín's house. The extremely brilliant dance of Pelele which begins the work; the *tonadilla*-like[1] phrases exquisitely set, the elegance of certain melodic turns, sometimes full of unaffected melancholy, sometimes full of uninhibited spontaneity, always refined and, above all, evocative, as though expressing the artist's inner visions, all this I have just recaptured in playing his music.

But how differently!

Then we were confident that success was near; the work

---

[1] The *tonadilla* is a light-hearted, popular dance.

was to have its première next winter at the Paris Opéra; nobody suspected that a cruel and unjust war would be sparked off a few weeks later by a neighbouring state which still described itself as a friend.

Now our wishes, our hopes, have been partly fulfilled. The opera has had its première, the success was great, but Paris did not witness it, and its composer – the victim of those who at that moment were still hidden enemies – could not share it with his relatives and friends in his country.

We who have been honoured by the composer's friendship and have admired his exceptional talent, must demand proper retribution for those who have wrenched away from us an artist who so brilliantly represented Spain abroad.[2] And after fulfilling that duty, both humanitarian and patriotic, we must unite to praise and to preserve as a treasure the heritage Enrique Granados left us when he died, the loftiest heritage a man can leave to his country: the product of his intelligence and his will.

[2] Granados.

IGOR STRAVINSKY
THE GREAT MUSICIAN OF OUR TIME

'La Tribuna', Madrid, 5th June 1916

THE RUSSIAN ballet, so magnificently directed by that noble artist, Serge Diaghilev, has arrived, at last, in this corner of Europe, transformed into a peaceful refuge by the saddest of circumstances. The company has announced and will carry out a programme in which music has a dominant place. And the composer who will conduct the Spanish premières of two works, *The Firebird* and *Petroushka* has arrived – Igor Stravinsky.

I am completely aware that this name is known to all those in Madrid who follow the progress of the arts in Europe, and even admired by many. But I wonder whether the anonymous mass that we might call the great public knows how important it is for us that so significant an artist as Stravinsky should revivify our polluted musical atmosphere with his art which, be it vigorous or subtle, is always fresh and clear. Does Madrid know that one of Europe's greatest artists is its guest? Will the city be able to reject the opinions of those who say that this composer's works will confuse the listener rather than lead him towards the truth? This, more than anything else, is what I would like people to know. Because Stravinsky's work is imbued with sincerity; the kind of brave, unbowed sincerity of one who says what he thinks fearless of what those who do not think or feel like him might say.

Stravinsky's music sometimes seems to me like a poster shouting defiance at timid people who will only follow a track that has been worn by several generations. Indeed, the composer of *Petroushka* wants to open up new paths or, at least, to renew the old ones, and the success of that avalanche of sounds called *The Rite of Spring* seems to justify his attempt.

Six years ago, when the same company which is now visiting us gave the première at the Paris *Opéra* of Stravinsky's first ballet – *The Firebird* – little was known about the composer. All that anybody knew was that he was a Russian, not yet thirty years old, and a disciple of Rimsky-Korsakov. Little enough information, but that première immediately placed him at the head of his generation in Russia and made him one of the leading composers of Europe. But admirable as that score is, the composer's musical personality was not fully revealed until a later season saw his *Petroushka*, the work brought to us by Serge Diaghilev today.

The sucess was immense. Musicians of integrity, particularly the younger ones, rejoiced in him as in a collective triumph. The others – the dishonest or the habit-ridden – growled and grumbled and turned away contemptuously. But they soon took their revenge. The occasion, a noisy one, was the first performance of *The Rite of Spring*. Their repressed rage erupted in the first bars and grew in a crescendo until the end. The same happened each time the ballet was performed. And yet each time the theatre was full, and each time the number of supporters increased. They fought real battles with the detractors, and it was even rumoured that the Austrian ambassador would protest at diplomatic level because of certain remarks made 'about him' by Maurice Ravel. A year passed, and the *Rite* was given again in Paris, not as a ballet, but as a concert piece. The success was great, clamorous, and the injustice largely put right. And those who had been violent the year before now timidly took refuge in a corner, lest the winner's revenge should take too practical a form.

Stravinsky had definitely conquered the Parisian public and *The Nightingale* – an opera in three acts, of a musical boldness which in many passages surpasses that of *The Rite of*

Spring itself – was received by the public with unanimous enthusiasm.

The four works I have quoted are the most considerable of those already known by Stravinsky. The première of the last one – *The Nightingale* – was given shortly before Europe was plunged into this cruel war. The great composer withdrew to Switzerland, and there he has been working on several pieces, among which two are for the theatre: *Le coq et le renard* (which he is writing for Madame de Polignac's puppet theatre) and *Noces villageoises* (a ballet for large chamber orchestra, eight solo voices and two choruses).

In the first of these two works the orchestra is much reduced, in the second it is of the greatest importance; in both the instrumentation is completely new. Each instrument has its own tonal and expressive function, and each string instrument has a separate part, never playing in unison. The dynamic impetus comes from those instruments that are by nature dynamic, for example trumpets, trombones and timpani. The other instruments create a web of pure melodic lines without the need for any support. It could be that in this work the idea of so-called pure music has come to life.

I have already spoken of Igor Stravinsky's artistic sincerity. This reveals itself, in a way perhaps unique in the history of music, in these three ballets and in *The Nightingale*. In these works Stravinsky employs means of expression that are completely new, and which exactly produce the effects he wants. Stravinsky's sincerity contains two qualities which determine the unity of his whole work: a very conspicuous national character, rhythmic and melodic, and the attainment of new sonorities. Let us follow this example, which is more valuable for Spain than for any other country, since the popular elements – traditional and religious – of Russian music are the same as those that have given rise to the songs and dances of our people.

Let us not forget, too, that Russian composers – Glinka and Rimsky-Korsakov among others – were the first to write Spanish symphonic music, and let us show Stravinsky the gratitude that we owe to the nation he so brilliantly represents by awarding him the admiration and the high artistic respect which his own work inspires in us.

INTRODUCTION TO THE NEW MUSIC

'Revista Musical Hispanoamericana', Madrid, December 1916

I SHOULD BE extremely unhappy if anybody were to consider any of my appraisals which follow to be lacking in respect for the great artists of the past. Nothing could be more alien to my intentions, or displease me more.

It is through works of art themselves that art progresses and takes shape. It has not been entirely the composer's fault if in certain periods of music history we have to note with regret a relative decline in quality – even in the works of the great geniuses. The milieu in which the works came to be written can have a negative influence as can other circumstances preceding the composition itself. The spirit of a particular age can come to dominate the strongest personalities who are then sadly blinded by a prevailing routine, succumbing to its spirit, not suspecting they had more than enough strength to overcome it.

This precisely is the glory of our own age, that many describe as great in order to excuse their own idleness. They do not seem to realize that the exertion of one's will, be it successful or not, has always been one of the highest virtues.

The new music has its origins in this effort to be delivered from old habits, to be free from shackles and from tutelage, to aim for the ideal state in which sound first unconsciously manifested itself as an art.

I wonder whether this ideal will ever be definitively fulfilled. Very probably not. But which human ideal will in this life? All we may and should aspire to is to discover, to decipher, the deeply hidden causes of things, in order to be able to enjoy their effects. This is the noblest way a man can occupy his intelligence and direct his activity, and this same impetus lies at the origin of science. Whenever this spirit is missing, art, believe me, has petrified.

Even more: every innovator in art has been, and is, considered a visionary, an eccentric, and what not. In order to be respected at least, the artist is required not to advance, not to endeavour to do more than the penultimate generation has achieved. Yes. The penultimate generation. The last, if nothing else, is suspect . . .

Why is it that the artist is excluded from the law of progress? It is a dark mystery, but a clear reality.

Furthermore, it sometimes happens that a new composer, having created musical devices to highlight and to perfect the melodic aspect of his work, presents the public with so ingratiating a work that not even the most difficult can deny its being so. In such a case the ill-disposed – to say nothing of the ignorant – critic will immediately criticize the pleasing elements in the work, encouraging his innocent readers to deride, and even to humiliate, the composer and those who have enjoyed his music. They say, for example, that this composer has only intended to surprise us with certain harmonies, which, though presenting now and then some interest, are not the product of an art aspiring to move us; of an art seeking to express deeply experienced, deeply felt states. This art, the eminent critic goes on to pronounce, does not aim either to be or to seem transcendental. (For him, as for many others, to be transcendental and to be unbearably boring amount to the same thing.) And he concludes his intellectual analysis by stating that the work in question can only be accepted as a curious instance of an art appealing solely to the ear – an art appealing solely to the ear!

I like the expression and that is why I repeat it. I have read it so many times with anger that I now find it amusing. . .

But really, I wonder whether this gentleman and others of this same mentality are innocent enough to believe that emotion is born in the sense organs. Let us take some comfort from the recollection that in his day Beethoven was thought to be mad, even stupid, and that Wagner was said to have had built a stone theatre for his cardboard music.

But do not think that the ill-disposed and the ignorant are the only enemies of new music. There are others as bad as they, or worse: those who believe and, with the best of intentions, go about saying that every new work – so long as it is written by a composer of established reputation – is admirable; that every new work, whatever the school, the tendencies and the ideals of its author, is the only one that can satisfy us, thus depriving of any merit the whole production of the past.

These estimable people, full of angelic naïvety, display an honours list in which a number of composers appear in total confusion – the more the better – men who would be enraged to see their names in conjunction. And this we must admire unconditionally.

These estimable people tell us, shuffling names with the most touching candour, that Debussy and d'Indy are César Franck's illustrious disciples and acolites; that César Franck was the founder of the French modern school, and that the members of this school and the Austrian, Hungarian, and Russian innovators are all the same under different labels; that Grieg was an absolute simpleton; that the only virtue of Chopin's music was its ability to alleviate the tedium of neurasthenic young ladies; that Mendelssohn's is not liked, and never could have been, except by sentimental British spinsters; that Mozart's – Mozart's! – hardly has any quality apart from a certain innocent gracefulness; and that the old Spanish polyphony can only prove useful in the treatment of insomnia; and to make it short and not try your patience any more, that Verdi was a follower of Wagner, and that both of them are destined to disappear. . .

It occurs to me now that you may perhaps be thinking, after all I have been saying, that you are reading the work of a superficial eclectic. Don't you believe it, for goodness sake. I do not have that kind of mind nor could I, being the person I am and thinking as I do. I consider eclecticism extremely harmful to the victory of any great idea. I wonder how an eclectic society could make any progress. And, therefore, I do not believe in eclecticism. He who accepts and applauds the most conflicting opinions, either has none himself – in which case he is good for nothing – or, if he has any, he is shy or indolent, giving the appearance of urbane and condescending agreement. I think we should never respect ideas opposed to our own. We have, of course, to respect the people who profess them, but nothing more.

And if the eclectic person is sterile, how valuable, on the other hand, is the unintentional collaboration of the most bitter enemies for the victory of the emergent cause! But it is high time to return to our subject, the only one I should have spoken about – new music.

Music is the youngest of all arts man has given birth to, since it did not become a conscious art form until the eleventh century. I refer to the form it has had ever since that time, and still has, meaning polyphonic music in the word's broadest sense, that is to say, music formed by two or more parallel melodic lines.

We shall now see how the musical present fuses with, in a certain sense, the remotest part, the natural principle of music. We shall see how, by virtue of our art's powerful spirit, the newest music appears simply to be a renewal of that earlier manifestation, forgotten for so long, but a renewal whose result is enriched by centuries of artistic evolution and experience.

In spite of rigid conservative elements, music will move further and further from academicism, from hollow rhetoric, from petty formulae. And those among the new composers with a truly creative spirit, will follow the others who have broken through to the path of truth and freedom leading to pure beauty, where music fulfils itself unaided.

Of course those same conservative elements, unable to bear patiently the progress of the new aesthetic ideals, rise against them, and contemptuously accuse them of decadence. Let us say at once that, from their point of view, they are right. For if they consider new music to be a continuation of the tradition they defend, the only difference being the use of certain devices which they ascribe to what ordinary people call fashion; and if they only see in the new ideals an accidental departure from tradition and go on thinking of it as the only real possibility, then of course they can justify their opinion that music is in a decadent state. But the mistake lies precisely in this way of reasoning, as the new music's spirit is so different from the one reigning in traditional music, that the one can by no means be thought of as a direct result of the other. And, thus, it is not difficult to gather that 'decadent' is a more accurate description for traditional than for new art.

Does it mean that the new owes nothing to the old? Not at all: it owes it a great deal, as I have more than once shown; but the debt refers to superficial elements rather than to the music's essence.

At this point I feel I must correct a recurrent error: namely, that the most typical feature of new music is the lavish production of dissonances. Nothing of the sort. I unhesitatingly declare that the spirit of new music could survive unimpaired not only in a harmonic work totally free of dissonance, but also in a homophonic piece (by which I mean a piece composed only of successive notes forming one single undulating line). Therefore, those who use certain dissonances, marrying them to melodies of traditional form and character, in order to make what they compose sound like revolutionary music, are committing a serious mistake. I shall never get tired of repeating that harmonic devices alone do not amount to the distinctive feature of new music; that the new spirit lies, more than anywhere else, in the three basic elements of music, namely rhythm, modality and melodic forms, the origins of feeling.

Does this mean that new discoveries in the field of harmony are of only relative significance? By no means, for they are of great value. That they are only one factor can be seen, for

B

example, in the music of Claude Debussy which shows a pronounced predilection for consonant chords. I mention Debussy because it can be affirmed, with hardly any risk of contradiction, that this experimentally innovating movement has its origins in his work. These avant-garde tendencies, of course, as in all other instances in man's history, were gradually fermenting in the works (and never in technical treatises) of other European composers. But new music's spirit, its aesthetic conceptions, and stylistic devices, were never affirmed in a precise, systematic, and definitive way, until the publications of the *Nocturnes,* the C major Quartet, *L'après-midi d'un faune, Pelléas et Mélisande,* and so many other works by means of which Debussy revealed to the musical world the new doctrine that was to become the starting point of an essentially new art.

The spirit of that doctrine, modified by Debussy's followers according to their individual and national characteristics, has generated works of such expression and evocative power, of such variety of feeling, as could never have been predicted.

You may think that in all I have just said there is nothing but an excessive proselytism that attempts to erase the musical past for the sake of the present. God forbid! And to prove I am not the victim of so absurd a bias, I shall pay homage to two of the greatest composers whose names, I am sure, have just arisen as symbols of indignant protest in the minds of my readers. I mean Ludwig von Beethoven and Richard Wagner, to whom the art of this century, as well as that of the last, are so much in debt. You can be sure that however great your admiration for those masters may be, it will hardly surpass my own. But with the same frankness I must tell you that, save for some exceptions I shall deal with later, their purely musical methods cannot be applied in a general way to works written by composers of other races without impairing their individual and national character.

I shall go still further: by following the musical formulae of Beethoven and Wagner with a servile attitude, even Austrian and German composers have come only to a standstill in the admirable and widely acknowledged progress achieved by their countries' music from the eighteenth century right up to the composition of *Parsifal*. This is so much so that, with the exception of Richard Strauss in Germany, and Schoenberg in Austria, it is very difficult – if not impossible – to find a composer whose works show any advance beyond Wagner's conquests, as far as form and technique are concerned. And even then the weight of tradition is so overwhelming to composers belonging to that race, that neither Strauss, nor even Schoenberg, has been able to free himself from it.

But I wonder what has caused this. I think it is easily apparent from a minute analysis of the works of Beethoven and Wagner. This will reveal to us that, except for Beethoven's *Canzona in modo lidico* and Wagner's *Parsifal,* in the works of these masters there is hardly a trace of earlier procedures. The huge musical heritage before Johann Sebastian Bach is systematically and voluntarily ignored or rejected, as though the art of sounds had not had an existence deserving consideration before the great Cantor. And as for Beethoven, we may very well suppose that in using the Lydian mode in his *Canzona,* he only intended to emphasize its religious character. For we know it was written as thanksgiving to the Divinity, (the word Beethoven used, surely influenced by the ideas of Robespierre, so much in vogue at that time), for having recovered from an illness. Beethoven was more or less a practising Catholic, and the Lydian is the fifth ecclesiastical mode in the series named 'authentic', and the third in the primitive series which preceded the Gregorian reform.

When we turn to Wagner, we find that although in *Parsifal* he used certain modal forms, and even certain themes from the Catholic liturgy, he never deserted the inquitous Protestant tradition that was the main cause, perhaps the only one, of the contempt classical musicians felt for music earlier than the seventeenth century.

This, I repeat, is the glory of our music: to have restored to art this forsaken treasure, profiting at the same time, in external devices, from the admirable teaching of past centuries. We should not be ruled by them, but we owe them our gratitude, for glimpses of the spirit of today's music were already to be caught in Haydn's *Creation,* in Mozart's *Magic Flute* and *Don Giovanni,* in Beethoven's *Pastoral* Symphony, in the works of Berlioz, Weber, Schumann, Schubert, Chopin, Liszt and, recently, in Richard Wagner's music dramas.

To this revered master we owe to a large extent the form of modern opera. Thanks to his example, composers who came after him rejected the absurd forms of Italy. Opera stopped being a series of arias for singers to show off their talents, and lyrical drama, in which the poem and the music form a unity, universally established and affirmed itself.

Yet Wagner was not the only reformer of music drama. We are also greatly indebted to a composer whose name is just beginning to be known in our country. I mean Modest Moussorgsky, the great Modest, as an eminent critic calls him, the brilliant Russian composer who in 1872, when he wrote his music drama *Boris Godunov,* drawn from popular themes, started the musical dramatic movement that has had overwhelming influence on European art. The new era in our music really begins with Moussorgsky. Thanks to him, as well as to Nicolai Rimsky-Korsakov, Balakirev and Borodin, the melodic forms and the ancient scales that had been rejected by composers and had taken refuge in the church, among the people, have been restored to great art. Let us not forget, either, that this resurgence has found a vigorous champion and propagandist through his writings as well as through his compositions, in my revered teacher, don Felipe Pedrell.

The spirit and tendency of that art which first became manifest in Debussy's works and continues with Stravinsky, runs through some of the admirable works of Paul Dukas and Florent Schmitt, through Erik Satie, who has in a certain sense been a harbinger, through Maurice Ravel, Isaac

Albéniz, Zoltan Kodaly, Béla Bartók, Arnold Schoenberg, Scriabin and others of less importance. In all these composers, whose techniques are in many cases totally conflicting, one unanimous aspiration, however, is to be found: to awaken the most intense emotion by means of new melodic and modal forms, of new harmonic and contrapuntal combinations; by means of haunting rhythms arising from the primitive spirit of music, which it now has and ought always to have retained, a magic art, through rhythms and sounds capable of evoking sentiments, beings and even places.

This art has abandoned the melodic forms prevalent in the seventeenth and eighteenth centuries, effective until about 1865, forms that were literary rather than musical, originating in most cases in the theatre aria and applied without exception to purely instrumental compositions. It has also abandoned more or less completely the only two modes used during three centuries: the Ionic and the Aeolian modes of the Greeks, that we commonly know as major and minor. Tonal superimpositions occurred, with one tonality prevailing. Music was not only given back the ancient rejected modes, but new ones were freely created that complied better with the composer's musical intention. The traditional way of thematic development was destroyed if it was not justified, and music's appearance was to be as the immediate result of its internal feeling; all this, within the areas established by rhythm and tonality.

It has also to be borne in mind that not all the composers we have named abide by the principle of tonality. Schoenberg's music in particular is atonal, and this extremely grave mistake must account for the dislike many of his works provoke in us. But it is not a widespread mistake, and fortunately most of the new composers respect the tonal laws, rightly considering them immutable.

One may ask which are the genres they prefer. The answer is that all of them are brilliantly represented in the newest art.

CONTEMPORARY FRENCH MUSIC

'Revista Musical Hispanoamericana', Madrid, July 1916

I THINK THAT the publication of G. Jean-Aubry's book, the Spanish translation of which I have the honour to present here, is of great importance at this time. For I consider that the horrible war Europe is going through, whatever the result of it, will be of use, amongst other things, in settling what we might call racial boundaries. These have been increasingly and constantly blurring, and together with them those values that characterize art created by a particular race. The point had been reached where such values, reflections of the autonomous spirit of each people, were becoming levelled and mixed in a sort of universal formula; music was not the least of the sufferers from that regrettable state of affairs.

The evil was all the more serious because those who were furthering the process either did not realise what was happening, or, if they did, they satisfied their scruples by boasting of a diehard nationalism. And if anyone pointed out to them that their deeds did not quite correspond to their words, they defended themselves by saying that the use of musical methods drawn from alien sources, far from being detrimental to a national art, exalted it with new· dignity. Such methods – they stated – are the heritage of the world; they have been created or systematically used by the greatest geniuses; they abide by untouchable laws and are therefore called classic. They may, of course, be elaborated and in certain cases, modified, but . . . woe betide anyone who attempts to break the sacred mould! And woe betide those who have dared to follow a different path, they will soon be forgotten, a just rebuke to their irresponsible pride, ignorance or aberration.

Thus have these prophets been speaking during the last thirty five years. After listening to them, many (almost everyone) submitted and followed them along the way that, according to those leaders, was the only possible one to reach the truth. Let us not forget that it was a broad and easy way. It amounted to nothing more than to follow in other pilgrim's tracks. Some however, a very few, let the caravan which was moving on tediously, pass by. They had not been convinced by such speeches; on the contrary, they fancied it to be an offence to those it was supposed to glorify.

Then they saw the field, wide and free, before them and, as though obeying a sudden inspiration, each one started to plough his own furrow. It was hard work, but faith was deep and hope growing. One ploughed near the old, well-known path, another a little further off, and some very far away. The last reached their objective first, some set off running across country, and nothing more was heard of them.

I have just told the parable of the history of new music in France. In G. Jean-Aubry's book you will meet those men of brave character, who suggest examples for us to follow. Some of the prophets are there too: Jean-Aubry is as well acquainted with them as with the others, the rebels, and he speaks of them all with the same respect, the same truthfulness. Each one appears according to his works which, whatever the intentions inspiring them, are always lofty, and have pursued no other aim than to make of France what France is today: the highest musical centre in Europe.

There is another benefit to be gained from this book: its author, who has been a friend of the most illustrious among French composers, deals not only with their works, but with their spirit, with their personal character, and with the tendencies prevailing in their work. This will destroy a serious error that has given rise in our country to the

regrettable confusion of presenting the names of certain
contemporary French composers *en bloc,* as belonging to a
single school. Here one learns that the aesthetic principles
upheld, and the methods used by the different groups of
admirable French composers are not only diverse, but even
radically opposed. Once and for all one will find out the
enormous distance dividing a Vincent d'Indy from a Claude
Debussy; a Gabriel Fauré from a Paul Dukas; a Maurice
Ravel from an Albert Roussel or from a Déodat de Séverac.
One will also learn that César Franck should never have been
considered as a French artist, not only because of his Belgian
birth, a fact in itself, but because neither his aesthetic doctrine
nor his technical methods, neither his preferences nor his
models, show the slightest relation to those features that
distinguish true French spirit and character – least of all in a
musical sense. The influence of César Franck and some of his
disciples on certain groups of French musicians was counter-
acted by the Debussyean reform, one of the most outstanding
processes in the history of contemporary music, considering
its consequences for musical art in France as well as
throughout Europe.

   In dealing with this point, I shall have to disagree
somewhat with G. Jean-Aubry's criterion or to extend it,
rather, for nobody attaches a greater importance to Debussy's
reform than Aubry, or admires the author of *Pelléas et
Mélisande* more than he does. I mean only that Debussy is far
more a restorer of the pure French tradition represented by
Rameau and Couperin. The times are over when, in order to
win respect for Debussy's work, one had to claim the support,
as it were, of names with a universal reputation.

   This is not unusual. Often we find in critical studies,
inordinate praise for particular old works, pronouncing some
equalities as definitive when, if anything, they should only be
considered as curious experiments. One hears people
effortlessly state that such a passage in such-and-such a
symphony or oratorio is a hundred times more moving than
anything written in our day.

To return from my digression. I was saying that Debussy's reform is one of the most important events in contemporary music history. I suppose many will think that I refer to the influence exerted by Debussy's aesthetic ideas, or even technical procedures, on certain composers who are therefore called Debussyean. I do not really mean that; the influence exists, but it is only relative, and even negative. A true artist must never affiliate himself to this or that school, however eminent its qualities. Individualism – at least I feel so – is one of the first virtues to be required from an artist. Nevertheless, any conscious and dispassionate judge of the renaissance taking place today in European music could hardly deny that Debussy's work emphatically marks the starting point. I quite see that some of the most important revolutionaries of the day adhere to aesthetic principles and even to certain procedures that are totally alien to those of Debussy. However, these new musical devices had never been used as they now are, in a systematic, positive, and sometimes almost exclusive way, before Debussy liberated music from its shackles and proved that in freedom it could live with as much logic, as much balance, as in the classical period; and as much perfection, or even more.

I shall go even further: there is no doubt that all the artists who followed him in his determination to win new forms and new means for music, based their speculations on the conquests Debussy had already achieved in either sense. When I speak like this, believe me, I am led only by a sense of strict justice; even supposing that I intensely disliked Debussy's music, my consciousness as an artist and an honest man would impel me to the same statements.

Still, it is not only the work of this master that leads me to claim for France a European homage towards the new music. Could I possibly forget the emulation aroused by the strong and varied work of a Paul Dukas; that his *Apprenti Sorcier* with its fantasy of sounds was the inspiration for so many admirable works. Or a Maurice Ravel, that uncommon artist who, after Debussy, was the great teacher in sculpting the precious material of music. Or Florent Schmitt, whose strong will attracted the unanimous admiration of spirits following completely opposite concepts. And indeed, it is hardly possible to speak of Ravel and Schmitt without mentioning the enlightened man who directed their studies, that musician of supreme serenity: Gabriel Fauré, whom I am very honoured to follow in the presentation of this book.

Were the space assigned to a preface unrestricted, I should add many other names. However, G. Jean-Aubry's book will speak for all I have just said and many other things. To pay homage to the new French music was its aim and that equally was the aim of Adolfo Salazar's translation, one of the few Spaniards bold enough to defend with a clear conscience and full conviction, the newest musical ideals.

Do not forget how very indebted to France young Spanish music is; how many of our artists, both composers and performers, found there a second mother country. Two of them – Ricardo Viñes and Joaquín Nin – are portrayed in this book with rare accuracy. Jean-Aubry has dealt with many others in different studies. He and Henri Collet have been the most persistent and effective propagandists of our music in France. From these points of view, and in the name of my country, I most gratefully greet them, and, furthermore, I would ask from the Government some testimony of gratitude towards these two great friends of Spain.

PREFACE to the *Enciclopedia Abreviada de Música* by JOAQUÍN TURINA[1]

Madrid, April 1917

THE PUBLICATION OF a book like the *Enciclopedia Abreviada de Música,* by Joaquín Turina, is a very unusual event in our country's musical life as, except for the writings of maestro Felipe Pedrell, there is hardly anything of such importance to be found. Even Eslava, who long ago proposed to teach us musical procedures by means of his then famous treatises, gave up that task when it was nearing its end, so that the last volume of his didactic works – which he intended to devote to the teaching of composition – was never published. The result is that, in Spain, musicians always speak about harmony, counterpoint and orchestration, but never about composition in the strict sense, save for the fugue.

Many years later, Turina comes to fill that gap: all those who are interested in the fortunes of Spanish music, must be intensely grateful. The talent and high artistic feelings this musician has so brilliantly shown in his creative works guarantee all he may tell us about the art of composition.

But I wonder how this book will be used by those aspiring to benefit from its teachings. Light can prove blinding for many who, having lived for a long time in darkness, now enjoy it for the first time. I firmly believe that art should aim only at generating emotion in all its aspects, and I fear therefore that somebody using the means as an end, will transform art into artifice, and think he is fulfilling his duty as an artist by treating sounds as a kind of chess problem, a

[1] A Short Encyclopaedia of Music.

hieroglyph, or some other innocent and useless pastime. It is true that some cannot do better; it would even be a gain if they could achieve as much. But I am not addressing them. I am speaking to those who know they have a creative capacity. I shall ask them to look towards the past – though without losing the ground others have conquered – to consider the admirable and constantly growing progress of this art since it was born; to admire, full of gratitude, those artists who, instead of following in the beaten track of their predecessors, have opened new ones; and to decide to imitate their example.

It is my humble opinion that the classical forms of our art should only be studied to learn order, equilibrium and an often exemplary technique. Their help should consist in stimulating the creation of new forms in which those same qualities appear, never in being copied (unless some other special formula is pursued), like a cooking recipe. To be fair, I must confess that in this book, not only the tendencies, but also the fruits of the new music are judged from a particular point of view that is not always mine. I believe that, nowadays, the main use of craft is to help us to make music sound so natural that it somehow seems an improvisation; but, at the same time, so balanced and logical, that the work as a whole, as well as in its details, reveals a higher perfection than that we admire in classical compositions presented to us until now as infallible models.

Is anybody thinking that all I have just said means that I shelter a more or less hidden disdain for the works of the past? So much the worse for me were it so. And so much the worse for those who, dazzled by the beauty of the new art, reject the old, for they would forgo exquisite joys, intellectual perhaps rather than emotive, but so great that they add to the pleasure of present-day music, by revealing in it the efforts of the past. All I was trying to say was that we should create without useless preoccupations, with joy and with freedom. Intelligence is only to assist the instinct, to channel and shape it, to tame it. But never to kill it, in spite of all the dogmas that stuff schoolbooks.

It is a fatal mistake to say that music has to be understood in order to be enjoyed. Music is not, and never should be, written for people to understand, but to feel it. In short, I believe art can be learned, but can hardly be taught. All those who, in artistic matters, endeavour to dogmatize, not only make a regrettable mistake, but also harm the art itself that with hidden pride they pretend to protect. Let every one then follow his own taste and tendencies; even if he does not amuse the others, he will thus at least amuse himself – no mean achievement. And furthermore, he who diverts himself in practising his profession, has a good chance of entertaining others as well.

To conclude: I consider all that is emotion in art as the artist's unconscious product, although he would never be able to objectivize it, to give it shape, had he not a conscious and perfectly accomplished command over his medium.

Therefore, when one has at one's disposal a work like Turina's for the study of composition, one cannot praise it enough. For beyond every difference of criterion, it is a precious instrument for a national artistic culture; if it is adequately employed, it can lead to abundant fruition.

OUR MUSIC

'Música', *Number 2, Madrid, June 1917*

THERE IS A RUMOUR going round that some pious ladies in Madrid are planning to raise money in order to offer the Berlin Caesar[1] a golden statuette of Martin Luther. Some time ago only a madman would have thought up something of this sort; yet at the moment it is proportionally less odd and preposterous than it seems at first, the world catastrophe caused by the will of one man having presented us with stranger things. And under such grave circumstances, how can we be surprised at some trifling contradictions in the little world of art?

If I say this it is because an exceedingly curious and interesting phenomenon is now taking place in Spanish music. Spanish composers have never shown before so deep a conviction of national values, yet never before have the critics (some at least) accused them, as they do now, of betraying those values.

But what is still more worth mentioning is that the models such accusers invite us to revere are – save for very rare exceptions – the result of the most obvious foreign imitation to be found in the whole history of European art. I, or rather, *they,* refer to our so-called *zarzuela grande* which, as anyone can establish with very little effort, is nothing but an echo of the Italian opera in vogue at the time of their composition. In a certain sense this is not wrong, for the dramas providing the plots for comic operas or *zarzuelas* could not possibly have a national character, most of them being only simple adaptations of foreign works.

[1] The Kaiser (Trans.)

Barbieri, wishing to 'hispanisize' our music, broke with that way of proceeding, as *El barberillo de Lavapiés* and *Pan y toros* so nobly demonstrate. But even in these sincerely national compositions, musical techniques very seldom remain uninfluenced by the Italians.

Only some time later, when Felipe Pedrell showed us through his works what the national way should be – a direct consequence of our popular music – did some honest thinking men propose following in the path opened by the distinguished master.

Please do not believe I am trying to reject everything composed during the period I have just been dealing with. Not only was it not my intention, but I have always expressed my admiration for a number of *zarzuelas,* be they *grandes* or *chicas,* which have been our chief musical activity for so long a period. Many of them will honourably survive in Spanish art, and the gracefulness of their melodies will hardly be surpassed by present or future composers. But between this fact and the declaration that the seasoning, as it were, with which these works are dressed, is purely national, there *is* a gap. Included in *zarzuelas* are songs written in a major or minor key (the *jota* or *seguidilla,* for example) that of course keep all their national characteristics. But surely our national treasure does not only consist of *jotas* or *seguidillas*? And besides, who will convince me that the rhythms of the *chotis,* of the waltz, or of the mazurka, with which those works are so generously supplied, are Spanish? I hesitate to criticize, and all I have just said is not intended to censure, but to be a statement.

Let us now turn to folksong. Some consider that one of the means to 'nationalize' our music is the strict use of popular material in a melodic way. In a general sense, I am afraid I do not agree, although in particular cases I think that procedure cannot be bettered. In popular song I think the *spirit* is more important than the *letter*. Rhythm, tonality and melodic intervals, which determine undulations and cadences, are the essential constituents of these songs. The people prove it themselves by infinitely varying the purely melodic lines of their songs. The rhythmic or melodic accompaniment is as important as the song itself. Inspiration, therefore, is to be found directly in the people, and those who do not see it so will only achieve a more or less ingenious imitation of what they originally set out to do.

I shall permit myself to advise all those wanting to compose strictly national music to listen to what we could call popular orchestras (formed by guitars, castanets and tambourines in my part of the world); only in them will they find that tradition they long for so much, and which is impossible to discover anywhere else.

I now realize I have not yet given my opinion, so kindly asked for by *Música,* about our contemporary symphonic music. Here it is, in a few words: I think this difficult genre is just entering a flourishing period among us. Our unforgettable Isaac Albéniz used to say that in a few years Spanish music would occupy a pre-eminent place in Europe. This generous artist was speaking in general terms, but I shall take the risk of particularizing and affirm that, in my opinion, symphonic music will be the most brilliant aspect of our output.

Since I have named Albéniz, I should like to pay homage to his memory, and to present him as an example of loyal and disinterested comradeship to all of us who are working towards the creation of a new Spanish art. Such an attitude is one more tradition to be established; whatever one's opinion, for art is freedom, let us respect people whose values are opposed to ours.

Without abandoning my feelings of genuine friendship I have nevertheless, to regret certain instances which are, alas, all too frequent. In these same pages I have read an article signed by my colleague, don Julio Gómez, who, pandering to outraged opinion in a manner I deeply lament, attacks a very prestigious composer whose work deserves all our respect. I am referring to Conrado del Campo. I mention the names because I like to speak out honestly. I hope that don Julio

Gómez – whose recent success I record here with pleasure – will agree I am right after re-reading his article; undoubtedly it was written in a moment of confusion, as surely excusable as any other human error. If he does agree, I shall feel completely satisfied, as a comrade and as an artist, for art is far loftier than the public's applause, however gratifying this may be.

II
DEBUSSY

.

DEBUSSY

IT IS NOT by chance that this essay on Claude Debussy was written in Granada: we are a thousand miles away from the earlier passions, in a region of pure and serene objectivity that was to make up the four-note tender tribute of the *Tombeau à Debussy*. He writes now with a more assured pen; no small achievement since Falla understood very well the implications of writing about Debussy in 1920. Thus, this essay seems to be the answer to those cool attitudes towards Debussy of post-war Paris.

Falla must necessarily have felt somewhat alien to this other Paris full of a violence that was strange to him. The anti-romantic reaction, the disgust with what had been the essence and apotheosis of music during the nineteenth century, also involved that most French of composers, Debussy. Already at the height of the war, in 1917, when Falla was proclaiming in the preface to the *Enciclopedia* the supremacy of emotion and instinct, Paris went in the opposite direction: that year saw the première of *Parade,* by Satie and Picasso, and a little later there appeared Cocteau's *Le Coq,* a manifesto against Debussyism at once brutal and delightful. To that time there also belongs the essay on pure poetry by Paul Valéry, where the allusions to music could still be considered a handbook of objectivism. Everybody, *Les Six* in the lead, revolved round Stravinsky, while he himself echoed Diaghilev by stating that everybody was centred on Impressionism. And, as a finishing touch for those years, Stravinsky's overriding words: 'I deem everybody was turning against Impressionism. And, as a finishing touch for those years, Stravinsky's overriding words:

'I deem music to be essentially incapable of expressing anything whatever: a sentiment, an attitude, etc. Expression has never been an immanent property nor the raison d'être of music.'

It is enough to look at the *Revue Musicale* – a perfect barometer of the music of its time – to realize that the anti-impressionist tendencies were reaching the very core of literary life. Writers (the echoes are to be found even in Giraudoux's *Maximes sur le sport*), were repeating other famous statements of Stravinsky directed against the Debussy school. 'Mystery', Michel Georges-Michel tells him, 'enhances music's beauty'. 'That', retorts Stravinsky, 'is a mistake. A naked body is always more beautiful than a clothed one. Art has been playing with mystery for far too long, and now it is necessary to denude music of mystery, as also painting, literature, and nature itself. Mystery is the unknown; let us have nothing unknown, and, above all, leave nothing hidden. Mystery belongs to Impressionism.' To denude music of mystery ... Can anything more perfectly anti-Debussyean be thought of? There is another testimony particularly interesting to us. Viñes told me that don Manuel felt a strong attraction towards Jacques Rivière's writings; in particular his 'correspondence of conversion' with Paul Claudel much impressed our composer. Jacques Rivière, an excellent music critic, was entirely formed in the school of Symbolism and Impressionism. However, after the end of the war he changed his tune: 'a tone of penitence', as he himself says, appeared. In the *Nouvelle Revue*, centre of literary interest, Rivière championed the same things as Stravinsky. He asked for a music 'toute en acte, un renoncement à la sauce, au charme', to do away with *claire de lune* and reflections in the water.

Not even Debussy's death could break this tight anti-impressionist front. Ravel and his better critics strove to point out the liberation from the impressionist language; Stravinsky produced a piece in homage to the dead composer as well as some parallel statements in a harsh tone. Even more striking: Alfredo Casella, the *enfant terrible* of contemporary Italian music, wrote beside Manuel de Falla's essay of homage: 'Nature – between you and me – is absolutely anti-impressionist: there is neither mist in our landscapes, nor mystery in our perspectives; there is always a sharpness of shapes, fine and implacably precise, an essentially classic light like that which illuminates the Hellenic Parthenon. This explains the deep gap between the present effort of young Italians and the Debussyist aesthetic'.

Now we have some elementary facts which help us to place Falla's essay on Debussy. Let us say, first, that of all the pieces that make up the *Tombeau* – by Dukas, Ravel, Roussel, Satie, Schmitt, Bartók, Falla, Goossens, Malipiero and Stravinsky – only Falla's has risen above the commemorative circumstances. Let us recall the deep, sharp and lyrical judgement of Joaquín Rodrigo: 'The influence of a strange instrument circulates through Spanish music, diluted in its veins and transmitting to them its uncommon beating; a gigantic, multiform and phantasmagoric instrument, idealized by the warm phantasy of an Albéniz, a Granados, a Falla, a Turina. It is an instrument that should have the wings of a harp, the hind quarters of a piano, and the soul of a guitar. And this soul takes shape for the first time in the homage of our great master Manuel de Falla to Debussy'.

Coming now to the text of the homage, let us point out, in the first place, its serenity: not one allusion to debates. By slightly forcing facts and dates, some have been tempted to contrast Stravinsky and Falla's preface to the *Enciclopedia* by Turina: I have been myself. Falla was very much in agreement with many of the postwar credos, but, as with Bartók, fundamentally he remained aside. The essay is about Spain, let us not forget its title, and our case is exceptional. Nothing has helped so much as Debussy's 'Spanish' music to liberate us from the picturesque, and even, Falla dares insinuate, from the excessively romantic and nationalistic documentary and modal fixations of Filipe Pedrell. This forms the heart of this most lucid essay. It is interesting to compare it, in the same issue of the *Revue Musicale*, with Cortot's comment on the works Falla analyses. They are separated by all the distance between 'topos' and discovery. Falla argues with 'Spanish music' manufacturers: catalogues were still full of 'Spanish Souvenirs' à la Moszkovski. He also argues with those at home, with the Europeanists at any price who turn away from Andalusia, or with those who consider her with the eyes and the ears of well-informed tourists. Sometimes a solitary phrase slips out as though he were an anti-Debussyean critic: 'the truth without the authenticity', referring to *Iberia*, is not pejorative. Thus the controversy is transcended. Falla, more than Bartók, saved what many professed to hate: that which García Lorca called 'duende'[1] when speaking about Falla's music.

Morever this essay gives us first-class evidence of Falla's aesthetic, best summarized in Debussy's proposition, far more literally achieved, as a symbol of contemporary music, in Stravinsky and in Falla than in his own music. 'It is necessary to adapt one's métier to the character one wants each work to have'. Falla expresses admiring agreement and this is not surprising: he was re-elaborating his aesthetic system, he was already bidding adieu to Andalusia and longing for Castile.

There is still something else of the utmost interest – the statement of Scarlatti's 'Spanishness'. This means that the fashion of stylistic revivals inaugurated by Stravinsky, finds in Falla the logic of an intense and essential nationalism. His revival does not seek form for form's sake, but for the essence of melody and rhythm. I think this incidental allusion to Scarlatti has enlightened the most decisive and creative horizons of the musical criticism of Adolfo Salazar, who was the protagonist of the homage to Debussy in the Sociedad Nacional de Música.

---

1 'magic'. (Trans.)

CLAUDE DEBUSSY AND SPAIN

*Published in the issue of the 'Revue Musicale' dedicated to
Debussy, Paris, December 1920*

WITHOUT KNOWING Spain, or without having set foot on
Spanish ground, Claude Debussy has written Spanish music.
He came to know Spain through books and paintings,
through songs and dances performed by native Spaniards.

During the last World Fair at the Champ de Mars two
young French musicians were to be seen going about together
listening to exotic music from more or less distant countries.
Unobtrusively mixing with the crowd, they absorbed the
magic of sound and rhythm the strange music contained.
New unexpected emotions arose in them. These young
musicians later on became two of the most famous names in
contemporary music—Paul Dukas and Claude Debussy.

This story explains the origin of many facets of Debussy's
music: the vast horizons of sound unfolding before him,
encompassing Chinese and Spanish music, made him
glimpse possibilities that were to be realized in fine
compositions. 'I have always been an observer', he used to
say, 'and profited from these observations for my work'. This
way he understood as well as expressed the very essence of
Spanish music shows how true this was.

Other reasons also helped his projects. We all know his
interest in liturgical music, on which Spanish popular song is
to a large extent based. Thus it is only too natural to find
frequently – even in works composed without any 'Spanish'
intention – modes, cadences, sequences of chords, rhythms
and even turns of phrase, that proclaim a strong kinship with

our true music. As proof of this I shall quote *Fantoches,*
Mandoline, Masques, the *Danse Profane,* the second movement of the Quartet, almost the whole of which could pass,
from its very sound, as one of the most beautiful Andalusian
dances ever written. And yet, as I asked the master about this,
he declared he had had no intention to give that *scherzo* a
Spanish character. Debussy, who did not actually know
Spain, spontaneously, I dare say unconsciously, created such
Spanish music as was to arouse the envy of many who knew
her only too well. He crossed the border only once, and stayed
for a few hours in San Sebastián to attend a bullfight: little
enough experience indeed. However, he kept a vivid memory
of the unique light in the bullring, of the astonishing contrast
between that side flooded by sunlight and the one in shadow.
In *Matin d'un jour de fête* from *Iberia,* perhaps an evocation is
to be found of that afternoon passed on Spain's threshold.
From this experience of Spain, his imagination moved further on. What he wanted was to concentrate on the evocation of Andalusia's spell. this can be seen in *Par les rues*
et par les chemins and *Les Parfums de la nuit* from *Iberia, La*
Puerto del Vino, the *Sérénade Interrompue* and the *Soirée dans*
Grenade. The last of these inaugurated the series of works
inspired by Spain, and it was a Spaniard, our Ricardo Viñes,
who first performed the work, as he did most of those by the
master, at the Sociedad Nacional de Música.

The intense feeling of Spain crystallized in *Soirée dans*
Grenade is something of a miracle if one considers that it was
written by a foreigner, led only by a brilliant intuition. We are
far away from those *Sérénades, Madrileños,* and *Boleros* which
the manufacturers of Spanish music used to give us. Here we
are actually given Andalusia, the truth without the authenticity, as it were, for although not a single measure is taken
from Spanish folklore, the whole piece, down to its smallest
details, brings Spain to us. We shall return later to this most
important fact. In *Soirée dans Grenade* everything is directed
towards one aim: the creating of atmosphere. We could say
that this music – bearing in mind what has inspired it – acts in

a similar way to the images reflected by moonlight on the limpid waters of Alhambra's many pools.

The same atmospheric quality is to be found in *Les parfums de la nuit* and in *La Puerto del Vino,* closely related to *Soirée dans Grenade* by the common rhythmic element of the *habanera* that, up to a certain point, is simply the Andalusian tango, and through which Debussy wanted to express the nostalgic song of Andalusian afternoons and evenings. I say 'afternoons' for what the composer was trying to evoke in *La Puerto del Vino* was the quiet and luminous time of the siesta in Granada.

The idea of composing this prelude was suggested to Debussy by a simple coloured photograph showing the famous monument in the Alhambra.[1] Decorated with coloured reliefs and shaded by high trees, it contrasts with a path full of light seen in perspective through the arch. The impression on Debussy was so great, that he tried to express it in music; and, indeed, a few days later *La Puerto del Vino* was finished. Related by its rhythms and its character to *Soirée dans Grenade,* it differs from the former by its melodic design. In the *Soirée,* we could say, the song is syllabic, whereas in *La Puerto del Vino* it often appears embellished with the ornaments peculiar to Andalusian folksongs that we call *cante jondo.* Debussy had already used this procedure in the *Sérénade interrompue,* as well as its outline in the *Danse profane,* showing his knowledge of the most subtle variants of our popular songs.

This *Sérénade interrompue,* which I do not hesitate to include among the works of the master inspired by Spain, differs in its rhythm, which is ternary, from the three compositions forming the already mentioned group, where binary form is exclusively used. As to this prelude's popular Spanish character, it is not superfluous to insist on the happy use of characteristic turns on the guitar that either precede or accompany the song; on the perfectly Andalusian gracefulness of the latter; and on the harshness contained in the challenging inflections following each interruption. This

music seems inspired by one of those scenes imagined by the
Romantic poets, which used to amuse us. Those giving the
serenade contend for the good graces of a lady, who follows
the incidents of the joust, hidden behind a grille full of
flowers.

We come now to *Iberia,* the most important work in the
group, and yet, exceptional in a certain sense, because of the
way the themes occur in the compositional process. The
initial theme gives rise to subtle transformations that
sometimes, let us not forget it, move away from the true
Spanish sentiment enshrined in the other works I have
mentioned. However, there is not the least criticism in this
observation; on the contrary, I think we must congratulate
ourselves on the new facet which *Iberia* discloses. It is well
known that Debussy always avoided repeating himself. 'It is
necessary', he said, 'to adapt one's métier to the character one
wants each work to have'. How right he was!

He also declared, on the occasion of *Iberia's* première, that
he had not intended to write Spanish music but, rather, to
translate into music the impressions Spain aroused in him.
Let us say at once that he achieved this most magnificently.
The echoes of the villages, in a sort of *sevillana* – the work's
generating theme – seem to float over a clear atmosphere of
glinting light; the intoxicating spell of Andalusian nights, the
joy of villagers who move forward, dancing to the sound of
guitars and bandurria band, all this sparkles in the air,
approaches, moves away, and our incessantly active imagination is captivated by a music intensely expressive and rich in
nuances.

I have not said anything so far about what these works
teach us by means of their harmonic writing, for this aspect
could only be dealt with by taking the whole group into
account. We know how much contemporary music owes to
Debussy, from this point of view as well as from many others.
Let us be quite clear: I am not referring to the servile
imitators of his music, I am referring to the direct and
indirect consequences of his work, to the feeling of emulation

it has stirred up, to the unfortunate prejudices it has destroyed once and for all.

Spain has greatly benefited from all these facts. We might say that, up to a certain point, Debussy has taken to new lengths our knowledge of the modal possibilities in our music already revealed by our teacher Felipe Pedrell. But while the Spanish composer to a large extent uses in his music the authentic popular material, the French master avoids them and creates a music of his own, borrowing only the essence of its fundamental elements. This working method, always praiseworthy among native composers (unless the precise documentary use is justified) acquires still greater value when practised by those who write music which is, as it were, alien. There is still another interesting fact regarding certain harmonic phenomenon which occur in the particular texture of Debussy's music. In Andalusia they are produced on the guitar in the most spontaneous way. It is curious that Spanish composers have neglected, even despised as barbaric, those effects, or they have adapted them to the old musical procedures. Debussy has taught the way to use them. The results have been immediate: the twelve admirable jewels left to us by Isaac Albéniz under the title *Iberia* are enough to show it.

I could say much more about Claude Debussy and Spain, but this modest study is only an outline of another, more complete, in which I shall also deal with everything that our country and our music has inspired in foreign composers, from Domenico Scarlatti, whom Joaquín Nin claims for Spain, to Maurice Ravel. But now I want to proclaim loudly that, if Claude Debussy has found in Spain a source of one of the most beautiful facets in his work, he has paid us back so generously that it is Spain who is today his debtor.

1 I suppose that must be La Puerto del Vino (the Gate of the Wine).

III

FELIPE PEDRELL

FELIPE PEDRELL

I SINCERELY BELIEVE that, if any orchestral conductor nowadays included in his programmes fragments from *Los Pirineos* or from *La Celestine*, something similar to what Falla describes in his essay would happen. Pedrell has not even gained the accolade of posthumous glory. Albéniz and Falla certainly paid tribute, but neither the public nor the critics looked into the reason for such a decline. Suffice it to recall the coldness present at the celebration of the first centenary of his birth, not long ago.

The source of this ingratitude is to be looked for in the constant leit-motif of contemporary Spanish music; namely, its isolation when compared with other cultural regions. We already have at our disposal, thanks to Pedro Laín Entralgo, an excellent collection of testimonies on the theme of Spain as it appears in the writings of the members of the generation of '98. Felipe Pedrell could very appropriately be included in the group, given his own attitude of protest; yet, this does not seem appropriate, for his long life has its roots that go back to the very heart of romanticism. Pedrell wanted to marry nationalism and universality, both seen through a romantic lens (the Russian group of 'The Five' may have been the model). His nationalism was decidedly romantic. It obeyed aesthetic premises clearly stemming from the historical school. It is significant, in this respect, that his nationalistic attitude led as far as making up a quotation of Eximeno. Let us not think it was a fraud of Pedrell, but an optical illusion

that made him see a strong outburst of nationalism in
Eximeno's disorderly sensualism. And his universality is
romantic too as he started – consciously or not – from the
Wagnerian movement, and Wagner was the most negative of
stimuli for national musical trends, as the case of Russia
shows. It would be interesting to indicate step by step the
importance of Wagner's influence on Pedrell, and the fatal
imbalance it carried for the composer's work.

We all go on repeating the truth that saddened Pedrell so
much: we see him as a scholar rather as a composer. Falla's
homage consists in focusing light on the heart of the matter:
what was really interesting in the genius of Pedrell became
apparent when he reached his pinnacle as a 'scholar-
composer' capable of stimulating Spanish music in a definite
way, with the *Cancionero*. Let us repeat for the umpteenth
time that Pedrell did not intend his *Cancionero* to be an
erudite work. Its very flaws, its 'modal' fanaticism, prove
that his intentions were those of a 'creator', not of a folklorist-
archivist. The whole work of Falla solves with genius the
great problem of nationalism, namely that popular elements
could become personal inspiration. This begins in effect with
Pedrell's *Cancionero*. And Pedrell plus Debussy's 'Spanishness' provide the necessary elements to understand where the
roots of Falla's creation originate.

This homage to Pedrell, which contained within it a double
attitude of fondness and irritation, is the best document of
Falla up to his sojourn in Paris. Falla, like Turina, like
everybody else, began dreaming of the theatre. The
significant expression, 'national opera' appears time and
again. His essay begins with a resolute criticism of the
zarzuela: the 'national opera' of Tomás Bretón was like it,
slightly larger in size and without the gracefulness of the
spoken passages. All that aspect of possible influence remains
completely aside. Falla rescues the only one that was to be
rescued, Barbieri. 'Two *zarzuelas* by Barbieri have a special
merit: *Pan y toros* and *El barberillo de Lavapiés*, for they evoke
the rhythmic and melodic characters of Spanish song and

dance at the end of the eighteenth and the beginning of the nineteenth centuries. These works exerted, beyond any doubt, a great influence on Spanish composers, giving our music, from the 1850s to the works of Isaac Albéniz and Enrique Granados, features that distinguish it from all the others.' Falla does not stress his admiration for the *género chico*, nor does he quote his *sainete* written for Loreto y Chicote, *Les amores de Inés*, because of his repugnance to that period, the period wittily christened by Gerardo Diego with the name of *Premanuel de Antefalla*. He could have emphasized more, it is true, his admiration for Chueca, as he would do later. It is a tactful gesture towards the dead Pedrell, who was deeply embittered to witness in Madrid the copious and easy success of those who did not ask themselves any questions. Some of us recall that delicacy of Falla in seeing Pedrell's centenary slip by while we were enjoying a discreet resurrection of *El barberillo de Lavapiés*.

It was still harder to deal with the ingratitude of Madrid towards Pedrell, which culminated in the discourtesy of the Real Academia de Bellas Artes. Falla tells it with anger, the formidable anger of a good man, and with many details. It was easier at that time to defend the picturesque motto *Wagner-Chapí* of Manrique de Lara. In Barcelona there was no decisive change in the lack of appreciation. Pedrell could have been more than an 'extra' in the outcry of Catalan separatism. He felt as if 'exiled' from Madrid, and his views always remained totally Spanish. Adolfo Salazar, in an obituary published in the *Revue Musicale,* to which we shall soon return, points this out very clearly: 'I do not see any possibility of Pedrell's works being staged in our theatres, unless political controversies come into play creating round his name a sort of regionalistic halo.' The warmth of tone in Falla's homage is easily explained by the fact that he wrote it at a turning point in his work, that is, together with the *Retablo de Maese Pedro*. Pedrell did not understand very well perhaps, as Salazar discreetly indicated, the need to redeem typically Andalusian elements. I wonder whether he could detect his own teaching amid the sensual impressionism of the *Noches en los jardines de España*. The festival of *cante jondo* at Granada was of course a different matter as its brochure was an exposition of Pedrell's principles; but Albéniz's *Iberia,* the *Noches* and even *El amor brujo,* were perhaps somewhat alien to Pedrell's feelings. When Falla turned towards Castilian music – the music Pedrell had rediscovered – it was a different matter. The February 1923 issue of the *Revue Musicale* includes a delightful note by Falla, the most poetic expression of his inclinations towards Castile. He speaks there of a concert given by Wanda Landowska at Granada, and he ends with these words: 'When, on that hill of Alhambra, we asked Wanda Landowska to play early music for us, our imagination was evoking the image of Isabel of Parma in the *Tocador de la Reina,* playing on her spinet the *Variaciones sobre el canto del caballero* by Félix Antonio de Cabezón.' This is also a tender homage to Felipe Pedrell.

In the November 1922 issue, the *Revue Musicale* includes the above-mentioned obituary notice by Adolfo Salazar, already confirmed as the only Spanish music critic to be considered as a disciple of Falla and capable of looking out at the European panorama tastefully and with sensitivity. He says the same things as Falla, although holding back on Pedrell's work as a composer. This article by Salazar has very great value, for besides announcing the completion of the score of *El retablo de Maese Pedro* and giving a tantalizing resumé of the premières in Madrid, it presents the immediate result of Falla's music: 'New French or Russian music was performed by several foreign artists: Cortot, Sauer, Brail-ovski, Rubinstein and the Hungarian Ember. The latter, after indicating a curious influence of Bartók on two young musicians born in Madrid, Rodolfo and Ernesto Halffter, played in his recital some works by them, whose talent seems to me very promising. By the side of some sedate and reflective pieces of an odd tonality by the elder brother, I should like to point out some other pages by Ernesto, full of vigour and irony, of such nimbleness and freedom that they approach the works of Stravinsky and of Poulenc, composers he worships. Ernest Halffter is seventeen years old; if I am not wrong, when he is twenty his gay and easy music will already have given him an excellent reputation.'

All these hopeful and promising things centre on Falla's essay on Pedrell, the first source of our knowledge of our contemporary music: from the *Cancionero* to the recitation of *Trujuman,* there is a link between two generations. This is the homage that makes amends for so many a Spanish literary figure's absence at Pedrell's commemoration. Don Manuel took his *Pedrelliana* to America. If this musical homage is now presented in the concert halls, Pedrell will have what he most craved for: his music played. Thus, the two homages are a perfect symbol of that different virtue called fidelity, cultivated by don Manuel like a good Christian.

For this edition we have used the translation Falla himself made in 1923, with some small changes in the order and in certain phrases, following notes he was preparing in the year of Pedrell's centenary.

FELIPE PEDRELL

Revue Musicale Paris, Febuary 1923

PEDRELL WAS A TEACHER in the highest sense of the word; through his doctrine, and with his example, he led Spanish musicians towards a profoundly national and noble art, a path that at the beginning of last century was already considered to be hopelessly closed.

I do not deny that certain nineteenth century compositions preceding or coinciding with the second and greatest period of Pedrell's output are worthy of respect and even, sometimes, of a certain admiration. Their authors excelled in one genre: the *zarzuela*. As this was, however, a mixture of Spanish popular tunes and Italian opera, it never passed national (or even local) borders. The musical substance of these works as well as their structure must irremediably be modest as they were generally written with insufficient technical training and in a great hurry. Their authors hardly pursued any artistic aim other than their prompt and easy staging and their equally easy understanding by the public. Whenever they tried to rise to higher artistic spheres (in the *zarzuela* called 'great', in opera, or even in religious music), except for some rare and illustrious exceptions, the result was a poor and puerile imitation of that Italian style which marks the beginning of the decadent period of that great musical country[1].

This was the state of things when the trilogy *Los Pirineos*[2] ('The Pyrenees') and the brochure *Por nuestra música* ('For our Music'), by Felipe Pedrell, were published. In them the author persuasively shows that Spanish lyrical drama, as well as any other musical work aspiring to represent us to the world, must find its inspiration on the one hand in the strong and varied Spanish tradition, and on the other in the admirable treasure left to us by our composers of the sixteenth, seventeenth and eighteenth centuries.

Pedrell unfolds his aesthetic theories in the above-mentioned brochure *Por nuestra música*, a complementary publication to the score of *Los Pirineos* that confirms them; since then, he has never failed to put those principles into practice.

His theories are based on an axiom enunciated by father Antonio Eximeno at the end of the eighteenth century, and according to which 'each nation must build its musical system on the popular song of its country'. Pedrell adds to this that 'the character of a really national music is to be found not only in popular song and in the instinctive expression of primitive ages, but also in the great masterpieces.' He then enumerates the indispensable conditions by which art becomes national; these are 'the uninterrupted tradition, the general and constant characteristics, the harmony between different manifestations, the use of certain native forms that an inevitable and unconscious power made suitable to the genius, the temperament, and the habits of the race.'[3]

The plan, as one can see, is forceful and overriding. As I have just said, the master abided by it since its drawing up, and so, more or less obediently according to their intentions, did the composers who created a most important part of that Spanish output that has characterized our musical revival.

There is something, in the way Pedrell put his plan into effect, which I should now like to refer to, for it is important as a universal aesthetic value.

Although Pedrell was very familiar with the works of our classics, and wholly devoted to them, his strength prevented him from being overwhelmed by their technical conventions. He followed a method, encouraged in him by his aesthetic ideal, thanks to which the devices he employed never went beyond their character as a means of helping towards the expression of musical essence. Nevertheless, what a wealth of possibilities is hidden in that seeming modesty, and what sustained depth of work is needed to reveal the harmonic mystery inherent in popular melody.

The composers of our golden age possessed that same simplicity when using expressive devices, even within the established forms. Excessive ornateness and useless complication have no affinity with the severely sober though expressive character of our best classical works. It is true that sometimes they betrayed that rule of moderation, but it is no less true that in many of those cases we see the emotional power impaired, as the music becomes more and more complicated.

This is a matter that deserves a study far deeper than the present occasion will allow me. What I have just said only tries to underline the fact that Pedrell always obeyed our purest aesthetic tradition – the tradition we should never deviate from, except when we are justified by precise and clear intentions. When I mentioned the absence of much ornateness in our music, I referred, of course, to polyphonic texture, for it is undeniable that Spanish music, be it ancient or contemporary, shows sometimes a considerable ornamental richness in its autonomous melodic lines, when these are inspired by certain characteristic phrases of Spanish folklore. But even this ornamental wealth is more seeming than real as it originates either in the adaptation of purely vocal inflexions to the fixed sounds of the tempered scale, or in the stylization of certain melodic-harmonic turns peculiar to our national instrument, the guitar, when played by the people. The most superficial study of those ornamental designs, and a comparison of them with those of other European schools, will be enough to convince one of that.

The beginning of the publication of the anthology *Hispaniae Schola Musica Sacra*, one year after *Los Pirineos* in 1894, the volumes of which have been enriched by monographs and analyses, meant not only that the master went on with his programme, but also that he succeeded in arousing abroad a growing interest in our classical composers. Thanks to that publication, the works of Cabezón, Victoria, Morales and Guerrero could be extensively studied and commented on by musicologists from all over the world, and so, in a later period, could other manifestations of Spanish music contained in the *Antología de organistas clásicos españoles* ('Anthology of Classical Spanish Organists') in *Thomas Ludovico Victoria Opera Omnia* ('Complete Works of Thomas Lewis Victoria') and in *Teatro lírico español al siglo XIX* ('Spanish Lyric Theatre Before the Nineteenth Century').

But meaningful as this proselytizing task was, it was only complementary to the complex revitalizing influence Pedrell exerted on contemporary Spanish music. He himself rejected, and justifiedly, the epithet of 'learned', by means of which some tried to divert attention from his personal *œuvre* to his work as a musicologist. We, on the other hand, who have been stimulated and guided by Pedrell's musical work, can affirm that it would have been enough of an achievement to have brought about, quite unaided, a renewal of Spanish music. But we bestow the highest importance on his actual teaching and on his making known once more our classic composers, both achievements having brought enlightenment and strength to his own compositions.

One can hardly conceive of a scholar-artist; but an artist who does not make use of his acquired scholarship to show off in his compositions, but tries to reflect in them the fundamental values that distinguish the nationality of his art, is fulfilling a very significant task. This was the case of Pedrell.

From *Los Pirineos,* his musical output reveals three basic qualities: a strong personality, a serene emotional strength, and an uncommon evocative power. If we study his work seriously we shall realize that these precious qualities originate, apart from the natural gifts with which God favoured him, in the assimilation of popular song and in the study of primitive musical art, which he transformed in free and modern expressive forms.

Pedrell himself related how in his childhood he applied himself to transcribing songs, street vendor's cries, and whatever music he heard, from the lullaby his mother sang to his younger brother, to the tunes of military bands. He began this laborious exercise at the instigation of his solfa teacher, and it became by far the most attractive of all games for him. Later, when he became a junior chorister at the cathedral of Tortosa, his native city, he had ample opportunity of practical initiation into the artistic forms of religious music. He also became familiar with the essence of those primitive songs still in use in some of our cathedrals. Tunes like the awesome *In recort,* quoted and transcribed by Pedrell in his *Cancionero,* filled the child's soul with tragic terror, as he put it. Knowing these facts, one cannot doubt that they contain the spiritual and artistic seeds of the musical work the young singer, after much travail, would achieve in his maturity.

I am not trying to make a study of Pedrell's output; I am simply trying to stress its great importance for our contemporary music, an importance so evident that only ignorance or bad faith could deny it. I am certainly not declaring that the music and aesthetic theories of the master are free from error. To appraise them may, as happens with every human work, give rise to reservations and objections quite proper if made fairly and with knowledge. Besides, not all his works are equally significant; those written before *Los Pirineos* can be regarded only as immature manifestations of the intentions leading to the brilliant result he achieved with that work. Nor did his later works find the same fruition. This could not be otherwise, since Pedrell lacked the experience that can be acquired only through practical artistic activity, through performance, the stage and the public. Nothing can replace this.

Nine years after the publication of *Los Pirineos,* and during the long period when he lived in Madrid, Pedrell composed *La Celestina*[4] and *El conde Arnau*[5]; these two works, together with the *Cancionero popular español,* form the rich heritage the master left us, and with them our interrupted musical history is resumed[6]. The period during which he composed the second and third of these works coincided with a decisive moment in my own life: it was then that I was taught by the master.

It seems that some of his old disciples have made it known that they did not gain much benefit from Pedrell's teaching. Perhaps they did not know how to profit from it, or they tried to find in it the opposite of the master's own deep-rooted aesthetic convictions. Perhaps they went to him without the technical training that is necessary when one seeks the advice of a great artist. As for me, Pedrell's teaching has been the artistic guide every well-intentioned apprentice needs so much.

Pedrell worked hard during his life. During the period I have been referring to, composition and musicological research represented only one aspect of his activity; he also taught music history and the aesthetic of music at the *Conservatorio Nacional,* and gave his courses on Spanish popular song at the *Escuela de Estudios Superiores del Ateneo.* Extremely interesting and fruitful, these had been preceded by equally memorable classes during which the master enthusiastically studied our musical treasure – religious and profane. Pedrell loved his art with a rare passion. 'The work of art', he used to say, 'is engendered by love; by our love of God, of our country, of our fellow men.' We shall see later how badly many of these fellow men rewarded these feelings.

Until the end of his life he kept this faith and this enthusiasm. Two months before his death – he was eighty-one years old and his health was shattered – he wrote to me on the occasion of the Andalusian primitive song competition:

'Tell your friends that I'm now singing *cante jondo* inwardly; if I'm not among you, I'll always be with you, and with all my heart.'

This last letter brings back to me his moral and physical image of earlier times. I see him in his working corner in Madrid (a mezzanine in the calle de San Quintín opposite the gardens of the plaza de Oriente), moved by some children's ring song coming in from the gardens nearby, or chatting in a friendly way with a blind singer of old *romances* or with a Galician bagpipe and drum player. How deep was his happiness when he told us of finding one of those old manuscripts in which the eternal characters of our art were revealed! How bright his look when he explained to us its qualities, drawing in the air a musical line with his finger!

I shall now say a few things about the master's last publication: the *Cancionero popular español,* a fundamental work that is like a synthesis of all his artistic creation. In it, a Spanish musician will find more than the manifold modal and harmonic values that emerge from the rhythmic-melodic substance of that music.

The mere comparison of some of the songs transcribed and harmonized by Pedrell with the transcription and the harmonization of the same songs appearing in preceding collections, will show us how a song that we hardly noticed before becomes singularly significant in his hands. The reason is that the very peculiar modal character of some of those songs is reduced in the older collections to the invariable tonal sentiment of the major and minor scales, whereas Pedrell extracted from them their true modal and harmonic essence.

But one of the main achievements of the *Cancionero* is to unfold before our eyes the evolution of popular song, and its technico-musical treatment in our primitive and classical art, that is, between the thirteenth and the eighteenth centuries.

This work – the last volume of which is still to be published – closes the master's musical activity. One can be surprised that this did not really come to fruition until the composition of *Los Pirineos*, finished by Pedrell when he was fifty-one years old. But this has very illustrious precedents as we all know: Cervantes published the first part of *Don Quixote* when he was fifty-eight years old. In both cases, the enumeration of the causes is as sad as it is convincing: the difficulties of earning their living, the lack of a state policy protecting certain artistic activities, and finally the monopolizing by more privileged or more pliable people, of the spheres of art.

For Pedrell was in his country a victim, not only of general indifference and lack of appreciation, but also of the ill will of many. When in 1904 he moved from Madrid to Barcelona because of his health, the Real Academia de Bellas Artes that some years before had felt honoured to receive him as a member, hastened to declare vacant his academic seat[8].

Furthermore, the Teatro Real in Madrid, which is our national lyric theatre, and therefore depends on the State, never welcomed any of his works. On one occasion some of his friends, (among them don Gabriel Rodríguez, father Eustaquio de Uriarte and don Rafael Mitjana, outstanding characters in more than one sense) succeeded in making the Teatro Real accept the opera *Los Pirineos*, the score having been 'previously approved' by the Real Academia de Bellas Artes. However although the work appeared on the programme of several seasons, it was never staged.

For dignity's sake I would not mention these facts, if it were not that a patriotic feeling compelled me to disclose them; not only to claim the honours due to Pedrell, but also to prevent such things from recurring in my country.

In spite of all this, Pedrell certainly obtained from his art during his long life, even in Spain, many well-deserved satisfactions. After the publication of *Los Pirineos*, soon followed by the magnificent anthologies *Hispaniae Schola Musica Sacra*, European musical circles began to focus their attention on Pedrell's compositions, which were already known thanks to the French translation of his manifesto *Por*

nuestra música. In France, Italy, Germany and Russia, critical
studies and articles were written on his own and his scholarly
work; at the same time Tebaldini conducted in Venice several
performances of the very important and admirable prologue
to *Los Pirineos*, played with great success by the members of
the Liceo Benedetto Marcello. Other performances followed:
in France, under the direction of Charles Bordes; in Holland,
given by the Bevordering der Toonkunst at The Hague. The
whole work was staged in 1902 at the Teatro del Liceo in
Barcelona, and in 1910 at the Teatro Colón in Buenos Aires,
in the composer's presence.

To this we should add the high esteem in which Pedrell was
held by cultivated people in Spain and abroad, as well as the
pride he felt when faced with the fruitful work of his more or
less regular disciples, (Albéniz, Granados, Millet, Vives,
Pérez Casa and Gerhard figure among them), and their works
in turn give an impetus and example to other Spanish
composers, so that they somehow followed Pedrell's teaching
without being his disciples.

Yet these very reasons for satisfaction exacerbated a latent
professional rivalry that eventually encouraged the voluntary
retreat in which Pedrell spent the rest of his life. He was seen
again in public only in 1911, for the festival Tortosa, his
native town, gave in his honour.

Since then, and continuing for many years, when the
moment came to plan the following seasons at the Teatro
Liceo, a desire was expressed to stage *Le Celestina*. But these
good intentions, never put into effect, were forgotten some
time later and so was the very existence of the great musician.
This reached such an extent that, when in 1921 Pablo Casals
included some fragments of *La Celestina* in the programmes
of the concerts he conducted in Barcelona, many in the
audience believed that it was a posthumous opera, many
others, that Pedrell was a Spanish composer of the
seventeenth century . . . When they discovered they were
wrong, the master's house was invaded by a crowd eager to
learn more about a man as good as resurrected. It seemed

natural that that performance should arouse a desire to know the whole work, and in its original stage form. Something, in fact, was said along these lines, but again good intentions were put aside, again piece and composer were forgotten.

This culpable consigning to oblivion, as well as the injustices I mentioned before, led the master – already nearing his death – to complain: 'Justice was never done to me, neither in Catalonia nor in the rest of Spain; they constantly tried to decry my qualities by saying that I was a great critic and a great historian, but not a good composer. It is not true: I am a good composer. I do not claim respect for my age, but for my work. Let them listen to it, let them study and then judge it.'

With deep devotion I transcribe his words; with them I close this filial homage that I offer to the memory of the man through whose works Spain has again joined the circle of Europe's musical nations.

NOTES

1 The figure of Barbieri stands out vigorously among the composers of that period. He was an exceptionally gifted musician, to whom we owe the publication of the *Cancionero musical de los siglos XV y XVI,* so often quoted and used by Pedrell. Two *zarzuelas* are Barbieri's most outstanding works for the theatre: *Pan y toros* and *El barberillo de Lavapiés,* which reflect the rhythmic-melodic character of Spanish song and dance at the end of the eighteenth century and the beginning of the nineteenth. Those works undoubtedly exerted an influence on Spanish composers, shaping certain unmistakable features we find in our music from about the middle of the last century until Albéniz and Granados.

2 Lyric trilogy in three scenes and a prologue, on a poem by Victor Balaguer.

3 Certain procedures of Pedrell, like the inclusion of musical passages taken from classical composers in some of his works, as well as the frequent use he made of popular works in their authentic form, are arguable, but they have nothing to do with the essentials of his theory; therefore they must be considered as purely accidental applications of that theory.

4 *La Celestina* (the author gave it the title *Tragicomedia de Calisto y Melibea*), in four acts, adapted from the play by Fernando de Rojas.

(The original play was in twenty-one acts, and therefore obviously not intended to be staged. Written at the very end of the fifteenth century, it is considered as the most outstanding example of a genre known as 'humanistic comedy'.) (Trans.)

5 *El comte Arnau,* lyric popular festival in two parts, poem by J. Maragall.

6 I only mention the works published after *Los Pirineos.* Among those still unpublished, although written by Pedrell during the same period, it is worth mentioning *Visió de Randa* (Ramón Llull), on a poem composed for the inauguration of the Palacio de la Música Catalana by Magín Morea, and *Glosa,* on a poem by J. Maragall (Orfeó Catalá, 1906).

7 I think it just to state here the name of don Juan Gisbert, a great friend and admirer of Pedrell, thanks to whom this work has been published.

8 It is true that to be a full member of the Academy it is necessary to live in Madrid, but it is equally true that in similar cases an accommodating solution has been looked for, and found. This was the case of Pereda, elected a full member by the Real Academia Española, although his usual place of residence was Santander. Pedrell's situation in the Academia de Bellas Artes facilitated a favourable solution as he was not a candidate, but already an academician. However, the statutes were scrupulously applied, and the fact is all the more significant because it was a colleague of the master who demanded it.

IV

INQUESTS

INQUESTS

(Nationalism and universality)

AS AN APPENDIX to these writings we include the famous brochure on *cante jondo*. It was not written by Falla himself. Apart from historical evidence the initial quotation from Hegel and a certain declamatory tone, incompatible with the master would enough to prove this. One can see quite easily in the brochure what stems directly from Falla's thought. The preceding essays on Debussy and Pedrell show this clearly.

I have included the brochure on *cante jondo* not only because of its rarity (the kindness of don Valentín Ruiz Aznar, an intimate friend of don Manuel, has made it possible for me to consult it), but also because it evokes that marvellous festival at Granada. Ignacio Zuloaga appeared together with Falla as a protagonist of the gathering. Both friends surely sought very different things, for their nationalities were different as well.

During those years, Falla's thinking was directed entirely towards the problem of nationalism and universality. Two notable circumstances converge on his compositions: his return to Castile, and the assimilation of the most advanced language of European music. Falla felt the need to reconsider for himself all the questions, and that when his own style was already formed, when he could have happily continued his Andalusianism. Again – could it have been otherwise? – he began to preach 'freedom'. In the statements Adolfo Salazar collected in *Sinfonia y ballet* we see how

Falla was on the alert to catch all that arrived from Vienna or from Stravinsky's Paris.

'Music can only be the expression of an individuality. No 'school' can write any music, but it can, instead, frustrate the individuality of young artists. Oh, young composers! I am already old enough to exhort you to speak freely, just as you feel. This freedom is the most difficult thing to reach, but then it is the only worth while thing securing.

'For the musician's heart, music is contained in everything: in people's appearance and in the intonation of their speech, in the colour of a river and in the silhouette of mountains within a landscape. That is why I am so strongly against Germanic formalism. Schubert and Mendelssohn undoubtedly have spoken according to their inspiration, but I cannot admit their art, or the art of anybody, is a stereotyped musical form. We also have our academic teachers in Spain, who force their disciples to write quartets in Beethoven's manner. But this excludes, of course, everything the young musician has to say, for the manner of a foreigner like Beethoven, or whoever, could obviously know nothing of the special music contained in the Spanish landscape, in the face or in the accent of our people, in the silhouette of our mountains. Such an exercise is only too likely to breed boredom.

'One should mistrust most nineteenth-century music; as for the classical symphonies or sonatas, one of the teacher's duties is to recommend every possible precaution against them. The freedom and the spontaneity of the eighteenth-century composers has been recovered only by the Russians and by Debussy. Music's grammar is not immutable, as classical Greek's is. The only means to study it is to follow its historic evolution.

'How stimulating to think of the future! For music starts moving forward precisely now; harmony has still to become artistic. For example, the folk songs of Andalusia are based on a far more subtle scale than that in which the octave is divided into twelve notes. All I can do, for the moment, is to give the illusion of those quarter-tones, by superimposing chords of one tonality on those of another. But the day is rapidly approaching when our notation has to be changed into another that conforms better to our needs.'

We want now to include the presentation of the Orquesta Bética de Cámara, where Falla's ideas on the use of instruments is summarized. The plan was somewhat quixotic. For if it was difficult to succeed in having in Madrid a chamber orchestra good enough to fulfil the double mission of 'rediscovering' pre-romantic music and of bringing the latest achievements to us, it seemed almost impossible to have such a thing at Seville. Falla, Halffter and Salazar, supported by a group of musicians, not only organized the orchestra, but had it make several tours all over Spain. This is the programme:

'Let us bear in mind that, from the time of early Italian composers until that of Mozart, musical production was divided, with very few exceptions, into three groups: church, theatre and chamber music. Therefore a concert by Vivaldi or by Bach, a sonata by Domenico Scarlatti, have the same right to be included in the category of chamber music as a quartet or symphony by Haydn or Mozart, since all those works were composed to be performed in private *salons*. Even symphonies are conceived of for a reduced number of instruments. It could be argued that those who play string instruments in a symphony are not soloists, like the members of a quartet. It is true, and that is why each section of the chamber orchestra bears a precise name. The number of performers of a trio, a quartet, a quintet and so on is established exactly, whereas for the concerto and the symphony only the balance between the different groups of the orchestra is essential, so that no one comes to dominate another. We know perfectly well how this balance was achieved in the period I have just referred to: approximately the same number of players were to form the string and wind sections. We also know that the great masters kept to the proper proportions when they composed symphonies, which explains the use they made of unison lines when they had to obtain superior power in the strings.

'Now, if we reduce the number of string instruments to that strictly necessary to achieve a balance, the individual work becomes obviously more intense than it is in a modern orchestra (the nineteenth-century orchestra, which is still for us the norm); with the increased responsibility of each individual, it is easy to realize how hard the preparation of a symphonic piece by a chamber orchestra must be. That is why I think it justified to call the members of the Orquesta Bética soloists, not only those who really are, as it happens, in the wind section, but also the string players, although they seemingly do not always have that role.

'All this refers to the eighteenth-century concert and symphony, but it can be applied to a most important part of today's symphonic production, as well as to certain works composed during the last century. Although written for a small chamber group, they are performed everywhere by the so-called great orchestras, in which the string section has had to be reduced in certain cases, at the express wish of the composers taking part.'

The other 'Inquests' we include give us a good image of don Manuel's maturity, of his restless and at the same time satisfying solitude. *El retablo de Maese Pedro* and the Concerto for Harpsichord had already had their premières. A gap of many years' silence intervened; Ernesto Halffter, the Orquesta Bética de Sevilla, projects about *La Atlántida,* hopes of composing a quartet . . . A new generation of poets were rising who understood the effort of Falla and the fruitful connection between nationalism and universality he sought. García Lorca freed himself from the picturesque with the help of don Manuel; the works of other poets were being set by Ernesto Halffter; the young 'poet-musician' Gerardo Diego also praised Falla, and Debussy's *Iberia* inspired his best sonnet which greatly pleased Falla. Azorin went to Granada and wrote about the town and about Falla; he made slight mistakes, but out of solicitude . . . It was a triumph: and *El sombrero de tres picos* danced by the Diaghilev Ballet turned it into an apotheosis.

STATEMENTS PUBLISHED IN THE MAGAZINE *Excelsior*

Republished in the 'Revue Musicale', Paris, July 1925

GRANADA IS THE town where I work, but unfortunately I travel too much, and when one travels one wastes time. Once a year I make 'a solitude cure' in a small town in Andalusia; during ten or twelve days I do not speak to anybody. Thus I prepare myself to work.

I completely devote myself to music, and music is a form of life, one has to carry it within oneself, because the formation process is somewhat like the creation of a being. It needs time, one sees it take shape in so natural a way. Music is so mysterious! I think music is the youngest art, and in two or three centuries it will become clear that we are now only at its beginning.

Social life becomes more and more complicated, that is why the artist must isolate himself. Music, unlike painting, has no primitive artists. The primitive character of eighteenth-century music is only relative, and besides, its values were lost, forgotten or depised, until the end of last century.

The essential elements of music, the sources of inspiration are nations and people. I am against music resting on authentic folklore documents; I believe, on the contrary, that one must start from the natural living fountainheads, and use the substance of sonority and rhythm, not their outward appearance. If we take Andalusian music as an example, we see that it is necessary to go to the very depths in order not to caricature it.

I believe in the beautiful necessity of music from a social point of view. It should not be egoistic but created for other people. Yes, to work for the public without compromising: this is the problem, this is my constant concern. One has to be worthy of the ideal one bears in oneself; it has to be expressed, even if it is difficult, even if one suffers, and then, the effort has to be concealed, as though the musical result were a very balanced improvisation, made with the simplest and surest of means.

ANSWER TO THE INQUEST
held by Musique,

Paris, May 1929

My models and my masters
All those who point out to me a path to be followed, in order to find and develop the technical means I need for what I have to say and do. I must add that this teaching is only relative, because a complete identity of ideas and of aspirations in art seems to me impossible.

My aspirations
Towards a strong and simple art, free from vanity and egoism – which is difficult to achieve.

Centres of attraction
a) A pure musical substance.

b) A music in which the eternal laws of rhythm and tonality, closely united, are knowingly respected. This is not said to blame those who act differently; on the contrary I believe that progress in the technique of an art, as well as the discovery of genuine possibilities leading to its further expansion, are frequently the result of seemingly arbitrary methods that later submit to eternal and immutable laws.

c) All that can be considered a renewal in the technical means of expression even if the results may not be, alas, always perfect.

Centres of aversion
Capricious dogmas, which become the worst enemies of true and unchangeable principles.

A mean-spirited nationalism.

The use of formulae considered to be 'of public utility'.

V

WAGNER

WAGNER

'*Il y a toujours un cas Wagner*'[1]

FOR MANY YEARS, Spanish intellectual life was centred round the *Revista de Occidente*. Its principal aim, which was to make known in Spain the most significant European developments, was not fulfilled in the field of music. There were at least a dozen books that awaited translation, above all there was the very existence of Spanish music. We can find in its issues, it is true, some important writings by Adolfo Salazar, for example 'La Música en tiempo de Goya', so neglected on the occasion of the centenary, notes by him and Gerardo Diego. I have always thought that the Spanish student of art lacked the knowledge of music he needed to understand properly the essence of the nineteenth century.

We do not want to recall here the internal history of the magazine *Cruz y Raya*, the hopes it first aroused precisely because of the greater attention it paid to what happened in Spain, and the later disenchantment due to its hapless policy. Manuel de Falla was among the editors, and in the sixth issue he published his important essay on Richard Wagner. Men of letters had widened their fields of interest: there was a 'poet-musician' like Gerardo Diego. García Lorca played his piano; Spanish Ballet, with la Argentina and la Argentinita aroused a meaningful response. *La corza blanca* had been published . . . The centenary of romanticism was about to be commemorated. Europe had grown weary of play and artifice and turned unconsciously towards music in which melody prevailed. Salazar spoke about Brahms and, as

---

[1] Nobody seems to know which enlightened mortal uttered this phrase

Ernesto Halffter said, these nostalgic memories stirred don Manuel's imagination. It was the right moment to speak about romanticism, to reopen once more the 'case Wagner'.

I do not think there were two more different spirits. Falla loved Chopin and Schumann, but I do not believe he ever felt at ease with Wagner. At the beginning of his essay he already avoids speaking about the human problem of Wagner, but he says enough. Then, serenely, he examines the music. Falla lived through the anti-Wagnerian reaction, contemporary with *Pelléas*; if he had been at Bayreuth when Stravinsky was there, his judgement would have been similar. But times had changed. Falla's favourite disciple, Ernesto Halffter, had conducted *Rigoletto* at Seville as if it were the most natural thing in the world, and did not conceal his admiration for Wagner. Some years afterwards he heard *Siegfried* at Bayreuth itself – entranced, I witnessed it.

Falla, like Ravel, thought Wagner beyond debate, a great musician and that it was necessary to come to terms with him. The solution he proposes in his essay reminds us of the famous verses Corneille wrote about Richelieu:

> 'Il a fait trop de bien pour en dire du mal;
> Il a fait trop de mal pour en dire du bien.'
> ('He did too much good to speak ill of him
> He did too much harm to speak well of him.')

The main thing was to place Wagner in the nineteenth century, which seemed to Falla a 'huge carnival'. Contemporary with this essay, is a book as important as it is unknown amongst us. Thomas Mann, himself an extension of the nineteenth century, places Wagner in his time, brilliantly putting him in line with Zola. Mann's thesis, to consider Wagner a great dilettante, is confirmed by Falla's description of how Wagner evolved his 'infinite melody'.

The core of Falla's essay is the criticism of Wagner's chromaticism. This corresponds perfectly well with the situation of European music ten years ago, when Falla and Stravinsky proclaimed separately the unchangeable principle of tonality. The atonality of the Viennese school is undoubtedly a consequence of Romanticism and Wagnerism. If Falla affirms that he prefers having to choose 'atonality' to 'pantonality', it is because, at that time, Schoenberg's very followers were already looking for a more stable order. This union of rhythm and tonality preached by Falla in agreement with Stravinsky – see the chapter Salazar dedicated to the reaffirmation of tonality in *La Música moderna* – was the theoretical expression of what he achieved in the Concerto for Harpsichord. It also meant a farewell to impressionism; what is enough for us is to understand the amount of asceticism, of renunciation that there is in the so-called 'Castillian Period' of Falla.

After criticizing Wagner's work as a whole, Falla rescues the musical miracles; all the chromatic furore is neutralized by the imperishable lyricism of *Tristan*. Even more, Falla affirms something to which not all French composers would subscribe: 'As to the craftsmanship, I do not think it has ever been a more perfect'; that fine craftmanship Ernesto Halffter always enjoyed so much. It was precisely in this quality that Ravel recognized Wagner's superiority over Franck and Brahms. And together with Ravel, with Roland Manuel and with Koechlin himself, whose nerves could not bear a complete Wagner opera, Falla affirms that Wagner was, beyond any other consideration, a great musician.

The essay on Wagner was written during the long period of silence stretching from the Concerto to the homage to Paul Dukas. We see the conscious reassertion of new paths leading to the completion of *La Atlántida*. We are surprised, however, by the preference he gives *Parsifal,* which he sees as Wagner's 'testament of faith'. Perhaps here we find echoes of Debussy's preferences – *Le Martyr de Saint Sébastien* and André Caplet owe much to *Parsifal*'s 'music' – or perhaps that monumental swan-song is better understood if one is conceiving a work of such great dimensions as *La Atlántida*. 'Il y a toujours un cas Wagner.'[1] When Falla wrote this essay, the Teatro Real was closed, so that one, two or more generations of opera lovers did not really know Wagner. After

the war, when *Tristan* was staged again at the Teatro de la
Zarzuela, when many teenagers fainted, all of us having been
exposed to impressive propaganda depicting Bayreuth as a
place of pilgrimage; when after the Berlin Orchestra and the
naïve but symptomatic Wagnerism in Barcelona, one had to
turn up with the alacrity of a fire brigade to soothe inflamed
hearts and nerves. For all of us, Falla's essay put the whole
phenomenon in perspective.

NOTES ON RICHARD WAGNER
ON THE FIFTIETH ANNIVERSARY OF HIS DEATH

'Cruz y raya', Madrid, September *1933*

I DO NOT THINK that in any other great artistic work success and error alternate as clearly as in Wagner's, nor that any has been as unfairly attacked, or as unconditionally revered as his. Neither his contemporaries nor the following generation were able to, or wanted to, free themselves from passion when judging Wagner's overwhelming work. No happy medium existed: they either denied the high, the very high, virtues, and the lesson enshrined in that music, or, shutting their ears to the voice of reason, they claimed that the very mistake that obscure and even sometimes destroy the qualities, were virtues. The case was still worse when the fanatic Wagnerian was a professional composer; incapable of reproducing what only genius can achieve, he clutched at the hope of becoming the master of the treasure he perceived shining through the many shadows, by copying what was false or wrong and therefore within the reach of anybody of normal intelligence. As to those who were not musicians, I have myself met more than one who was demonstrably shocked at the slightest criticism of his idol.

Now, after half a century, we look at Wagner in a very different way: his works live an independent life, and, although full of the force of the master, they do not have that prophetic sense he aspired to give them. In fact, for us they are quite the opposite. We consider them to be eminently representative of the period in which they were written, the music as well as the text. This was precisely Wagner's great failure: he wanted to lay the seeds of the music drama of the future, and from the harvest only his own music remains, and then that part better suited for the concert platform than for the stage. (An exception is that part of his dramatic production where the lyricism and atmosphere more or less conceal those structures of the past he intended to replace.)

I do not intend to write from a human, rather from a musical point of view, the former being fatally subject to fashions, feelings and tastes. All that had to be said about Wagner's aesthetic principles, about his exacerbated romanticism, about his philosophic ideas, and so on, has already been said. Therefore, if this essay contains something which appears to be along these lines, it will be for strictly musical reasons.

Although Wagner strongly yearned for a transcendental ideal, as we all know, he only followed this inclination when it did not upset his egotism. A consequence of this was the mixture of strength and weakness shown by his life and by his works. We do not have to deal with his life, except for the facts concerning his art. To be fair, whenever I listen to Wagner's music, I try not to think of him. I could never abide his arrogant vanity nor his proudly immature determination to embody his characters; he believed himself to be Siegfried, Tristan and Walther, even Lohengrin and Parsifal. That was typical of his time. Wagner, like so many others of his stature, was a gigantic character in that gigantic carnival better known as the nineteenth century, to which only the European War put an end (and thus inaugurated the great asylum our own century is proving to be).

Some of the influences exerted by Wagner's art on the music of his time are still active. This is one of the main points I shall deal with; in his music we are obliged to point out not only the qualities, but also the fundamental errors previously mentioned, trying to restrict their influence (still alive half a century after Wagner's death despite intervening reactions). Let it be clear that I am not trying in the least to diminish the achievement of this great composer. When I mention his

errors I shall weigh my words scrupulously, aiming
benefiting future artists, never at the expense of my own
tendencies or preferences.

Wagner frequently avoided obstacles and whenever
blocked followed strange paths leading into some dark jungle.
There is only one exception to this rule: it seems that he never
permitted himself to sacrifice to the music whatever in the
already published poem might have proved an obstacle. This
example of honesty is worth pointing out in these times when
more serious commitments, publicly contracted, are eluded
for the sake of hidden purposes.

But let us return to the music. Perhaps in this particular
instance we find the cause of what many have interpreted as
Wagner's excessive preference for his literary creations.
Whatever the real reason, it is necessary to confess that,
although the rule was very laudable, the way in which Wagner
solved its inherent problems was not always exemplary. If the
hindrance resisted too much, he yielded to an easy but fatal
solution. A proof of this is his famous invention of an infinite
melody (melodic sequences without tonal limits); this, with
all due respect to conscious mistakes, is only one of those
brilliant sleights of hand which since the eighteenth century
have been attempts to substitute for truth.

The first of his dogmas beyond discussion is that which
required the internal union of rhythm and tonality; only by
holding to this eternal principle can the musical devices
become powerfully stable. Let us not forget that music
develops in time and in space. To perceive effectively time
and space, it is essential to determine their limits, to establish
the initial, central and final points, or the points of departure
and suspense, linked by a close internal relation. Sometimes
this relation apparently blurs the tonal sense established by
its limits; but it is only for a short time and with the intention
of underlining that very tonal value, which becomes more
intense when it reappears after having been eclipsed. We
should not forget either, that it is necessary to be fully
convinced of the fundamental truth offered by the natural

acoustic scale in order to establish the harmonic – and
therefore contrapuntal – basis of the music, as well as to give a
tonal structure to a series of melodic periods which, being
generated by the same resonances which integrate that scale,
have to move at different levels. What I mean is that the
intervals forming that column of sounds are the only real
possibility for the constitution of the chord, as well as an
infallible norm for the tonal-melodic construction of those
periods that, limited by cadential movements, compose every
musical work. We can affirm, then, that in those natural
principles, fully dependent on rhythm, the whole of music is
contained. These forces, measured movements and acoustic
resonances, generate all the other elements of art: modal
scales, disposition and development of the vocal or instrumental parts, etc. And the very word of the text, which
shares the origin of melody, must obey those principles in
order to acquire a musical value. But we shall not be able to
use these essentials of music efficaciously if we do not
constantly watch over the degree of potency determined by
the close approach or the withdrawal of their initial point, and
if we do not determine the limits of future periods leading to a
final point or to a point of voluntary suspense.

And that was what Wagner, who accurately adhered to the
laws in the imperishable part of his output, deliberately tried
many times to elude, shielding his musical heterodoxy behind
the reasoning his philosophical dilettantism inspired in him.
In those moments, he abandoned his steady, vigorous pace
and entered the dark jungle, creating a constant instability
that at the beginning is only a disturbance, whereas at the end
it imperceptibly deflects our attention.

This tendency found an easy development in an excess of
chromaticism and in an inexorable sequence of enharmonic
modulations; the whole of the obvious effects of this was
called pantonal music, a pompous notion that matches well
with other, more fundamental errors of that century, the
results of which are still active.

For myself, I rather like to be told things clearly; that is why, having to choose, I decidedly prefer the chronologically new atonality to that of pantonality. For what happens here happens with every bad example: as it is very easy to imitate, it is followed even by those who reject what the composer's personality stands for.

The essential truth I have affirmed could of course be refuted; it is well known that almost every aberration can be rationalized and defended. It is a human frailty to accept evident errors for fear of being despised by the powerful people who propagate them. Musically it is unnecessary to say that chromaticism and pantonality, like every other artistic device, consciously used can not only be legitimate, but also excellent, provided their use is not the result of too easy a system, but of the reasoned choice of expressive means. Wagner himself proves this in *Tristan,* where the chromaticism (frequently tonal, anyway) finds its appropriate function as a spontaneous expressive force.

At the beginning of this essay, I said that Wagner's work, unique in music and the other arts generally, shows us where right and wrong can occur, thus stimulating us to seek truth and avoid error. For example, the subservience of his music to certain alien purposes compels us to be fundamentally concerned with the defence of music's rights. His pretentious vanity in wishing to eliminate everything inessential; his tonal and melodic restlessness lead us to observe a more serene and strict discipline, whereas the lack of personality of the instruments in the orchestra – admirable in other respects – drives us to isolate and enhance the timbres. His irksome verbosity and his exasperating dramatic realism urge us to strive after conciseness and after a simple, though intense, musical expression. His passivity towards certain nullifyingly overwhelming influences of his time, impels us to take precautions against those of our own epoch.

Where the positive effects of his music are concerned, they are so great and clear, that to state them may seem superfluous to those familiar with the master's work (and these pages are principally meant for them). The marriage of singing and of lyric declamation with the expressive value of word and concept, are among the most outstanding achievements of his art, and as for the craftsmanship, I do not think there has been any more perfect. With the development of the leit-motifs, he reached admirable heights, in spite of their excessive use; a subtle example of his skill to transform a motive is the orchestral beginning of Siegfried's monologue in the wood. This aspect of Wagner's art has value as a rich collection of examples of the techniques of variation.

To Wagner's effort we owe much of music's progress in liberating itself from dead formulae. In many cases his reforms were positive, and even of permanent value, but they were not the only possibilities, as many held who were not musicians. Wagner's art was great, even in its mistakes, and splendid when it abode by the eternal principles: who does not remember the overture to *The Mastersingers*?

Much was said with regret about the influence of Wagner's conscious nationalism on many composers of other races, sometimes opposing his own. This is evident, but I have always thought that Wagner's example, if followed in its positive aspects, not only is not pernicious, but provides a vigorous incentive for all to try to reflect in their own work the characteristic genius of their own nation and of their race.

In *Parsifal*, that eucharist-like play, Wagner's aspiration towards the pure ideal reaches its fulfilment, after appearing unmistakably in many of the poems he later set to music. And let us not forget an appealing facet of his nature; he never sacrificed his art to easy profit; he was never mean. It is true that he incessantly hunted for money, but as a means to achieve his noble artistic aims or his less noble human aims, never to amass it.

I also wish to mention his stubborn firmness, a true example for us, with which he strove for the fulfilment of his purposes, as well as the zeal with which he constantly strove for high standards in music theatre.

Nobody could equal Wagner in endowing the dramatic action with a most propitious musical atmosphere. In this sense he was more than an extraordinary artist: he was a prophet. This quality becomes most apparent when his ardour arouses our highest aspirations. This is the merit of some pages of *Lohengrin* and many of *Parsifal,* that clear testament of faith, of Christian redemption, that Wagner, nearing the end of his life and yielding to a pure impulse of his unruly consciousness, set in opposition to past misdeeds. That act of faith shows itself not only in the deep emotion called forth by the music for the sacred scenes, but also in the way the religious texts of the poem are imbued with love and reverence; the whole frequently inspired by the Catholic liturgy itself. That is doubtless why for me *Parsifal* is one of the most sublime works of art ever achieved in spite of the conscious tonal disintegration that frequently affects the music.

In these pages I have tried to pay tribute to the art and genius of Wagner on the fiftieth anniversary of his death. Something, or much, in my words may have gone against my purpose, yet I think, with Quevedo, that it is not enough to feel what one says; one also has to say what one feels.

Note on Tonality

I believe it can be defined as follows: Melodic form (a series of consecutive sounds, joint or not) that, based on an acoustic scale, forms a musical concept. To this initial form or tonality subsequent ones which constitute every musical work must submit by means of modulations, that is, transposition of the initial tonality one or more degrees higher or lower.

VI

RAVEL

RAVEL

BETWEEN PROSE AND verse written by young Andalusians in the pages of the honoured magazine *Isla,* Falla published his tribute to Ravel. It is his last essay, I believe, for from America only short and somewhat forced journalistic statements reached us. From a literary point of view this article is a model of tenderness and serenity, a model of elegance. Falla says what Ravel would have liked most, what he concealed from shyness or pride.

De Falla's essay leads us directly to pre-war Paris; perhaps since don Manuel retired into solitude, he only remembered that time, when he had been almost happy. Pre-war Paris of the thirties – Dukas dead, Viñes depressed, Ravel living through a sad sleep of the mind – was quite different. With news of Ravel's death arriving during the lonely difficult days of the Spanish war, memories became essential to continued life; in these circumstances Falla wrote his homage.

Through it we learn that Falla knew Ravel's *Sonatin* before going to Paris – the first Spanish performance of this *Sonatine* was given years later by Gabriel Abrue at the Sociedad Nacional de Música. Then we read the name of Ricardo Viñes; Viñes told me many times what the meeting of those two very shy men was like: their silence overwhelmed by the flamboyance of Viñes himself, who was in his golden period of 'premières' and folly. This meeting took place at the time of the *Rhapsodie espagnole* which was set up against Rimsky-Korsakov's *Caprice* as being genuinely Spanish, while a deserved eulogy of Chabrier's *Espagne* was written.

On the basis of Ravel's Basque   his Spanishness has become a 'topic'. Falla,   from the *habanera*, explains Ravel's creative process very well. Those paragraphs, together with the essay on Debussy, are the most reflective and complete identification of the Spanish theme in French music. Ravel's search for Spanish rhythms has a vigour, a force, and a sharpness, quite different from Debussy's 'evocation'. The heated controversy on Ravel's Debussyism can be perfectly well settled by comparing *Iberia* with the *Rhapsodie espagnole*.

The core of Falla's essay is levelled against the obsession of seeing in Ravel only the craftsman and the creator of pastiche. Falla wants to bring to the foreground the inspiration; he has recourse to such words as the 'prodigious child', a more beautiful formula than the 'old child' of Tristan Klingsor. The essay is dedicated to Roland Manuel, biographer of Falla and of Ravel. It has the tranquility of a·farewell.

NOTES ON MAURICE RAVEL

To Roland Manuel and Maurice Delage

'ISLA', Jerez de la Frontera, September 1939

I HAVE ALWAYS THOUGHT that Ravel, far from being the *enfant terrible* many saw him as during the period when he first revealed himself as an artist, represents the exceptional case of something like a 'prodigious child' with a miraculously cultivated spirit who works spells through his art. This is the reason why his music cannot always be judged without knowing the sensitive personality it so exactly expresses; the critic can miss the truth, to the point of denying his music any emotion, when in fact it pulsates with a candidness sometimes disguised under a wistful or playful irony. It is an audacious art, supremely refined and uniquely perfect, in which the composing methods, closely linked with the choice of musical means, always obey the creative intention; an art that reveals not only mental activity, the fruit of study and of experience, but also something that nobody can acquire simply, being beyond conscious capacities. That is why we can gratefully predict, without reservations, that Ravel's music will live forever among those who follow similar paths.

I met Ravel a few days after my arrival in Paris, in the summer of 1907; this was the beginning of a heartfelt friendship. I then knew only his *Sonatine* which I had heard in Madrid and which had strongly impressed me. Some time later, when I could realize my constant desire to go to Paris and get in touch with my favourite composers, I wanted from the very first moment, to meet Ravel. This proved easy, thanks to Ricardo Viñes, brave champion of that avant-

garde who had urged me to go to Paris. He welcomed me most
warmly; attracted by his prestige this flattered me as a
Spaniard. I did not suspect then that I would soon owe so
much to his art and to his strong friendship. I think back
feelingly of these first times in Paris where I had gone with no
fixed plan, but which became for me an extension of my own
country.

But let us return to the day on which I met Ravel for the
first time. He and Viñes read through the *Rhapsodie
espagnole,* which Ravel had just published in its original piano
version for four hands, and which they were to play for the
first time at a concert of the *Nationale.* The *Rhapsodie,*
besides confirming my impression of the *Sonatine,* surprised
me because of its Spanish character. This coincided with my
own intentions – unlike what Rimsky had done in his *Caprice*
– for it was not achieved through the simple arrangement of
folklore material but rather, except for the *jota* of the Foire,
through a free use of rhythmic, modal-melodic and ornamental elements of our people's song; and these elements did not
alter the composer's own manner, although they were applied
to a melodic language so different from that of the *Sonatine.*
Certain objections raised by Viñes as to practical difficulties,
certain passages arranged for a four-hand performance,
prompted Ravel to orchestrate the original version – a plan
soon and splendidly carried out. Thus he began the admirable
series of transportations of piano works for orchestra that
show unsurpassed talent and virtuosity.

But how was I to account for the subtly genuine
Spanishness of Ravel, knowing, because he had told me so,
that the only link he had with my country was to have been
born near the border! The mystery was soon explained:
Ravel's was a Spain he had felt in an idealized way through his
mother. She was a lady of exquisite conversation. She spoke
fluent Spanish, which I enjoyed so much when she evoked the
years of her youth, spent in Madrid, an epoch certainly earlier
than mine, but traces of its habits that were familiar to me still
remained. Then I understood with what fascination her son

must have listened to these memories that were undoubtedly intensified by the additional force all reminiscence gets from the song or dance theme inseparably connected with it. This explains not only the attraction exerted on Ravel, since his childhood, by a country he so frequently dreamt of, but also that later, when he wanted to characterize Spain musically, he showed a predilection for the *habanera*, the song most in vogue when his mother lived in Madrid. This was the same time that Pauline Viardot-García, famous and well acquainted with the best composers in Paris, spread the *habanera* among them. That is why that rhythm, much to the surprise of Spaniards, went on living in French music although Spain had forgotten it half a century ago.

The case of the *jota* is different. Used in France with the same function as the *habanera*, it still possesses in Spain the vitality it had in the past. I do not think any Spanish composer has ever succeeded as Chabrier has, in achieving so genuine a version of the *jota*, as it is shouted out by the people of Aragon dancing in rings at night.

The art of Ravel, far from being made up only of skill and ingenuity, as many still affirm, reveals the hidden force that drives it. His choice of latent harmonic resonances, as well as his orchestra, so limpid, so full of vibrations, would be enough to deny the impassive nature that his appearance might suggest, and that could only have been an unconscious reserve of character. I shall not insist on the fine sensitivity of the 'prodigious child', which glows in his melodic expressiveness – a sensitivity equally manifest in the unmistakable accents and inflexion of his lyric declamation. All I want to say is this: whoever has seen him at crucial moments of his life cannot doubt the emotional capacity of his spirit. I shall never forget how clear this became to me when his father fell critically ill. After an urgent pilgrimage through Paris we went back to his house where, realizing there was no hope, he implored me in an anguished tone to go and fetch our friend the abbé Petit – also dead today unfortunately – to give his father the Christian sacraments. The good and quiet soul of

Ravel broke out only in such circumstances, never in his music, forged in some inner world that was a refuge against an intrusive reality. How else could we explain that works like the Quartet, *Gaspard de la nuit*, and *L'heure espagnole* had been written when their composer was going through a difficult time! I can see his extremely modest study, and feel how it contrasted with the precious quality of music that Ravel revealed to us on an old piano as modest as the whole room.

When I think of the projects that an artist I admire announced, and that death made impossible for him, the grief and loss becomes heavier. Amongst them he showed a strong preference for one in particular when he spoke to us about it; this was approximately at the time of *Daphnis*. I refer to a *Saint François d'Assise*, a part of which he managed to sketch: that of the sermon to the birds. It is a pity that the need to finish occasional urgent works has deprived us of a composition that could have been, thanks to that pure and serene expressiveness so peculiar to Ravel, the most Franciscan, perhaps, the saint has so far inspired. I take comfort from imagining it through Ravel's other works: the Quartet for example, distant in time from that project but not in spirit, and in which, by a happy coincidence that seems rather an act of fate, there are echoes of the carillon at Assisi. And as to *Ma mère l'oie* ('Mother Goose'), I sometimes suspect that for the second part and for the finale, which has so beautifully religious a character, Ravel may have used some of the sketches for that *Saint François,* which, however, would have been so welcome for that man who in his youth was called *Il Francesco* because of his love of that country.

Fortunately the strong French character of Ravel's art is unanimously acknowledged, even when applied to exotic subjects. It would really be difficult to deny it; whereas, in order to accept it, it is enough to pay attention to his melodic phrases, markedly French in sentiment as well as the very special features due to certain favourite intervals. But Ravel's style, so firm and delicate in its boldness, so clear, orderly and precise, offers us another outstanding quality: the absence of vanity. This virtue is the more noteworthy if we recall that Ravel composed most of his work at a time when, under strange influences, music was required at least to affect a certain haughty aspiration to what was thought to be transcendental. I think that the composer's refusal to yield to such requirements reveals a rare discernment.

APPENDIX

Cante Jondo

Its origins. Its values. Its influence on European art

Anonymously published on the occasion of the first competition of *cante jondo,* organized by the Centro Artístico de Granada: Corpus Christi, 13th and 14th June 1922.

EL "CANTE JONDO"

(CANTO PRIMITIVO ANDALUZ)

SUS ORÍGENES. - SUS VALORES MUSICALES. SU INFLUENCIA EN EL ARTE MUSICAL EUROPEO.

Se publica con motivo de la celebración del 1.ᵃ Concurso de "Cante Jondo, "organizado por el Centro Artístico de Granada. -:- Corpus Christi. 13 y 14 de Junio de 1922.

EDITORIAL URANIA GRANADA

Portada del folleto sobre el cante jondo

I Analysis of the Musical Elements of *Cante Jondo*

(a) *The Historic Factors*

Three factors in Spanish history have influenced to a different degree the general life of our culture, and have an obvious relevance to our music history: the adoption by the Church of Byzantine chant, the Arab invasion, and the settlement in Spain of numerous groups of gipsies.

The great master Felipe Pedrell writes in his admirable *Cancionero Musical Español:* 'The persistence of musical orientalism in various Spanish popular songs is the deep-rooted result of the influence exerted by the most ancient Byzantine civilization which brought into being those formulae peculiar to the rites of the Church of Spain from the time of the conservation of our country to Christianity until the eleventh century, when the Roman liturgy was introduced'. We would like to add that in one of the Andalusian songs, the *siguiriya,* which we believe best preserved the old spirit, we find the following elements of Byzantine chant: the tonal modes of the primitive systems (which must not be mistaken for the modes we now call 'Greek', although these are sometimes an element in the structure of the others); the use of enharmonic intervals typical of primitive modes, that is, the division and subdivision of the interval between the seventh degree and the tonic considered in its tonal function; finally, the absence of a metrical rhythm in the melodic line, and its wealth of modulating inflexions.

These characters are likewise present in Moorish Andalusian song, the origin of which is much later than the adoption of the Byzantine liturgical music by the Church of Spain. This is why Pedrell affirms that 'our music does not owe anything essential to the Arabs or to the Moors, who probably reformed only some ornamental features common to the oriental and the Persian systems, whence their own stems.

The Moors, therefore are those who have been influenced'.

In making those statements we shall suppose that the master was referring only to the purely melodic music of the Andalusian Moors, for it is true that in other forms, especially in dance music, there are rhythmic and melodic elements that cannot possibly be traced back to the primitive liturgical chant of Spain.

One thing is beyond doubt: the music that is still known in Morocco, Algiers and Tunis, as 'Andalusian music of the Moors of Granada' not only has a personal character that distinguishes it from other species of Arab origin, but also in its rhythmic dance forms shows the origin of many of our Andalusian dances: the *sevillana,* the *zapateado,* the *seguidilla,* etc.

In addition to the liturgical Byzantine and Arab elements, the *siguirilla* contains forms and characteristics that are somehow independent from the primitive sacred songs of the Church and from the Moorish music of Granada. Where do they come from? In our opinion, they derive from the gipsy tribes who settled in Spain in the fifteenth century. They came to Granada, where they generally lived outside the city. They gradually integrated themselves with the people, until they were called by a name that shows to what point they had been incorporated in the civil life: *castellanos nuevos,* being thus distinguished from those of their race in which the nomadic spirit survived: the *gitanos bravíos.*

Those tribes, who arrived from the East, according to the historical hypothesis, give Andalusian singing a new character which consists of the *cante jondo.* This is the result of all the factors we have mentioned, not the product of one of the coalescing tendencies. The original Andalusian element fused and shaped a new variety in conjunction with the received influences.

All we have said will become clearer if we analyse the musical features of the *cante jondo.* This name is given to a group of Andalusian songs, the genuine type of which we believe to be the so-called *siguiriya gitana*; from this stem other kinds, still alive among the people – the *polo,* the *martinete,* the *soleares* – which, thanks to their very high qualities stand out among the great group of songs the common people name *flamenco.* Strictly speaking, this name should only be given to the modern group formed by the songs called *malagueñas, granadinas, rondeñas* (the last one being the origin of the other two), *sevillanas, peteneras,* etc. All these varieties can only be considered as a consequence of the former group.

Before underlining the purely musical value of the *siguiriya gitana,* we should like to point out that it is perhaps the only European song which preserves in all its purity – in structure as well as in style – the highest qualities of the primitive song of oriental people.

(b) *Relationships with primitive oriental songs*

The essential elements of the *cante jondo* present the following analogies with some of the songs of India and of other oriental countries:

1. The use of enharmonic intervals as a modulating means.

'Modulating' is not used here in its modern sense. We call modulation the simple movement from one tonality to another that is similar but on a different plane, without however changing the mode – major or minor. This is the only distinction made by European music, from the seventeenth century until the last third of the nineteenth. These modes or melodic series are composed of tones and semitones, the position of which is immutable. But the primitive Indian systems and those deriving from them do not consider that the places the smallest intervals occupy in the melodic series (i.e. the semitones of our tempered scale) – the scales – are invariable. In those systems the production of intervals that inhibit similar movements obey a rising or a lowering of the voice, which originates in the expression given to the sung word. This is the reason why the primitive modes of India were so numerous, for each one of those which were theoretically determined gave origin to new melodic series by freely altering four of its seven sounds. This means that only three of the notes of the scale were invariable. Moreover, each of the notes that could be altered was divided and subdivided, so that in certain cases the starting and finishing notes in some fragments of phrase were altered, which is exactly what happens in the *cante jondo*. To this we must add the frequent practice in Indian songs as well as in ours, of the vocal *portamento*, that is, the way of leading the voice so as to produce the infinite nuances existing between two joined or distant notes.

Thus, the way in which the word modulating is used, to denote the manner of a singer's using his voice as a means of expression, is far more exact in this case than in that to which the conservatoire treatises of European musical technique refer.

In summarizing this, we can affirm that in the *cante jondo*, as well as in the primitive Eastern songs, the musical scale is a direct consequence of what we could call the oral scale. Some theoreticians even suppose that word and song were one and the same thing in their origin. Louis Lucas, speaking about the excellence of enharmonic music says, 'that it is the first to appear in the natural order, by imitation of the birds' song, of the animals' cries, and of the infinite rumblings of matter'.

What we now call 'enharmonic modulation' can be considered, in a certain sense, as a consequence of the primitive enharmonic genre. Yet this consequence is apparent rather than real, because our tempered scale only allows us to change the tonal functions of a sound, whereas in the actual enharmonic process that sound is modified according to the natural needs of its attractive functions.

2. *We recognize as peculiar to the* cante jondo *the usage of a melodic field that seldom surpasses the limits of a sixth.*

This sixth, of course, does not consist only of nine semitones, as in our tempered scale; through the use of enharmonic intervals, the number of sounds the singer can produce is substantially increased.

3. *The repeated, even obsessive, use of one note, frequently accompanied by an upper or by a lower appoggiatura.*

This is characteristic of certain enchantment formulae, even of the kind of recitation that we could call prehistoric and that leads some people to think, as we pointed out before, that song preceded other forms of language. In certain songs of the group we are considering, (particularly in the *siguirilla*), this device permits the destruction of every feeling of metrical rhythm, and thus gives the impression of sung prose, although the text is in verse.

4. *Although gipsy melody is rich in ornamental features, these are used only at certain moments – as they are in primitive Oriental songs – to express states of relaxation or of rapture, suggested by the emotional force of the text.*

They have to be considered, therefore, as extensive vocal inflexions rather than as ornamental turns, although they sound like the latter when they are 'translated' into the geometric intervals of the temperate scale.

5. *The shouts with which our people encourage and incite the 'cantaores' and 'tocaores' also originate in a habit still to be observed in similar cases among the Oriental races.*

It must not be thought, however, that the *siguiriya* and its derivatives are simply songs that have been imported from the East. At the most, it is a grafting or rather, a case of the coincidence of origins that certainly did not reveal itself at one particular moment, but that is the result, as we have already pointed out, of an accumulation of historical facts taking place through many centuries in our peninsula. That is why the kind of song peculiar to Andalusia, although it coincides in its essential elements with those developed in countries so far away from ours, shows so typical, so national, a character, that it becomes unmistakable.(1)

II Influence of These Songs on Modern European Music

(a) *Russia*

The excellence of natural Andalusian music is demonstrated by its being the only one which foreign composers use in a constant and fruitful way; the songs and dances of other nations have also been employed, it is true, but mainly, if not exclusively, with regard to their characteristic rhythms.

Many of those rhythmic forms have brought forth compositions of the highest artistic quality, as has also happened with some old European dances (like the gigue, the sarabande, the gavotte, the minuet, etc), but their number is small and besides, only a couple of those purely rhythmic values represent each country.

Our natural music, on the other hand, has not only been a source of inspiration for many of the greatest modern composers abroad, but also of enrichment of their methods of expression, since they found in Andalusian music certain very high musical values that had been systematically preferred by composers of the so-called classical period. This is the reason why modern composers (defining them as composers since about 1850), did not limit themselves to borrowing only one determined element from our music; they used absolutely all of them, provided they could be adapted to the temperate scale and to the usual notation. This influence was directly exerted by the Andalusian *cante,* the main trunk of which is the *cante jondo.* Here are some facts which confirm our thesis.

Referring to Michail Ivanovich Glinka and to his long sojourn in Spain, don Felipe Pedrell says in his *Cancionero Musical Español:*

> '... Later he stayed for two years in Madrid, at Granada and at Seville. What did he look for there, wandering about by himself in the quarter of Avapiés or along the street of las Sierpes? The same thing he looked for in the Albaicín at Granada, when he was

captivated by the guitar playing of the famous Francisco Rodríguez Murciano, an artist of a musical imagination both ardent and inexhaustibly inventive. Glinka eagerly sought his acquaintance and they soon became friends. One of the greatest pleasures for the great Russian composer was to sit down for hours and hours, listening to Rodríguez Murciano while the player improvised variants of the accompaniments of *rondeñas, fandangos,* Aragonese *jotas,* etc., and writing his inventions down carefully, in order to transcribe them for the piano and the orchestra. But this determination of Glinka was useless; fascinated, he turned towards his friend, listening to the sounds he produced: a torrent of rhythms, of modes, of flourishes that resisted every attempt at transcription . . .'

Those observations and studies determined the creation of certain orchestral devices that enhance the value of *Souvenir d'une nuit d'été à Madrid* and of *Caprice brillant sur la jota aragonesa* composed by Glinka during his sojourn in Spain.

But however significant these notices may be, they do not suffice to show how important the influence of Andalusian music was on most of the members of the group of 'The Five', the direct heirs of Glinka. Other aspects of our music, especially of the old Andalusian music, aroused Glinka's interest during the two years he spent in Spain. However admirable the art with which Rodríguez Murciano played the Spanish songs and dances on his guitar, it was only one instrumental performance of them, among many others. We must suppose that Glinka would not miss any of the occasions that were offered to him, to enrich his notebooks with the *reflections* (since in most cases he could not achieve more than that), not only of the songs and of the dances collected directly from the people, but also of the accompaniment with the guitar, the castanets, the tambourine and the clapping hands. All the more so, as all of that was intensely alive in the milieu in which he constantly lived during his long sojourn in Spain. The songs of the *cante jondo,* the most cultivated at that time (1849), were to exert the strongest influence on 'The Five'. The affinity existing between the *cante jondo* and an equally important group of Russian folk song being strong, the comprehension and assimilation of our songs by these composers must have been most natural and spontaneous. Our art aroused in those musicians a great appreciation of the charms and rhythms of their own, the sequel of which was the forming of an intention to incorporate into artistic music the blending of the characteristic elements of both groups of songs and rhythms. The result was that unmistakable style which is one of the highest values of Russian music at the end of the last century. We are sure that all those who know the output of Rimsky-Korsakov, of Borodin and of Balakirev, to name only some of the most illustrious, will agree with us.

The influence of the Andalusian folksong on Russian composers is far from being an obsolete affair. Less than a year ago the famous Igor Stravinsky, a guest of Andalusia by then, was deeply impressed by the beauty of our songs and dances, and announced his intention of using them in a future composition.

(b) *France*

Russia was not the only country to be influenced by our people's music. Another great musical nation was to follow her example: France, represented by Claude Debussy. Although many French composers preceeded him in that direction, their intentions did not go further than to make music *à l'espagnole;* and even Bizet, in his admirable *Carmen,* does not seem to have set himself any other aim. Those composers, the most modest as well as the most eminent, were contented with the often false lead offered to them by this or that collection of songs and dances, the national authenticity of which was only granted by their authors' having a Spanish name. And since that name was not always, alas, that of a true artist, the document frequently lacked every value.

Such conduct could not satisfy a man like Claude Debussy. That is why his music is not composed *à l'espagnole* but *in Spanish* or rather, *in Andalusian,* the *cante jondo,* in its most authentic form having inspired not only the works he intended to have a Spanish character, but also certain musical values that are present in other pieces, not composed with that intention. We refer to the frequent use of certain modes, cadences, unions between chords, rhythms and even melodic phrases, which show an evident kinship to our natural music. And yet, the great French composer had never been to Spain, with the exception of a few hours spent in San Sebastián to attend a bullfight. He acquired a knowledge of Andalusian music by attending very frequently the sessions of *cante* and *baile jondo* given in Paris by the *cantaores, tocaores* and *bailaores* who went there from Granada and from Seville on the occasion of the two last world fairs.

Is there any better argument to show the great importance of our *cante jondo* as an aesthetic value? For we should not forget that the work of that 'prodigious wizard' called Claude Debussy is the point of departure for the deepest revolution ever in the history of music.

Debussy's attitude towards our music is not an isolated case in modern French composition. Other artists, especially Maurice Ravel, have used many essential elements of Andalusian folksong in their works. Ravel is also one of those who were not contented with making music *à l'espagnole*. The part of his work in which he used elements of Andalusian musical language, intentionally or not, shows very clearly how profoundly Ravel assimilated the purest essence of that language, transposing it, of course, into his own style.

As to what Spanish composers owe to the *cante jondo,* irrefutable proof is given by the works of some of the signatories to the request for support and protection for the *cante jondo,* presented to the municipality of Granada. We could add many others, and we should do so, if we did not fear to cause omissions, involuntarily but fatally, because of the wealth of Spanish works that owe their existence, and very often their success, to the more or less direct use of Andalusian music, and to the features it suggested.

III   The Guitar

To finish these notes we should like to point out the extremely important role played by the Spanish guitar in the influences to which we have referred.

The use of the guitar made by the people represents two clearly determined musical values: the rhythmic value, external and immediately perceptible, and the purely tonal-harmonic value.

The first of these, together with some cadential phrases of easy assimilation, was the only one to be used over a long period by more or less artistic music, whereas the importance of the second, the purely tonal-harmonic value, was hardly recognized until relatively recently; the only exception being Domenico Scarlatti.

The Russian composers we have mentioned before were the first, after the admirable Neapolitan musician, to take note of it; but as the only one of them to know directly the way of playing peculiar to the Andalusian people was Glinka, the artistic application of it was inevitably small. Glinka himself paid more attention to the ornamental forms and to some cadential phrases than to the internal harmonic phenomena that take place in what we could call the *toque jondo* ('touch jondo').

It was Claude Debussy who incorporated those values in artistic music. His harmonic writing, his texture, prove it in many cases. Debussy's example had immediate and brilliant consequences; one of the best of them is the admirable *Iberia* of our Isaac Albéniz.

The *toque jondo* remains unrivalled in Europe. The harmonic effects that our guitar players unintentionally achieve are one of the marvels of natural art. Even more, we believe that our fifteenth-century instrumentalists were probably the first to add a harmonic accompaniment (with chords) to the vocal or instrumental melody. And let it be clear that we do not refer to the Moorish-Andalusian music, but to the Castilian; we should not mistake the Moorish guitar for the Latin. Both of them are referred to by our authors of the fourteenth and the sixteenth centuries, and what they say proves the different musical use of each instrument(2).

Pedrell affirms in his *Organografía musical antigua española* that the Moorish guitar is still in use in Algeria and in Morocco; that it is called kitra (khitara > guitarra?); and that the strings are plucked. The primitive way of playing the Castilian guitar is to strum it, and this is still often heard among the people. That is why the use of the Moorish instrument was and is, melodic, like the lute and the bandurria, whereas the function of the Spanish-Latin guitar was harmonic, because if one strums the strings, only chords come out. Many will say that those chords are barbarian. We affirm instead, that they are a marvellous revelation of unsuspected possibilities of sounds.

The Cante Jondo Competition

(Primitive Andalusian song)

THE CENTRO ARTÍSTICO DE GRANADA, aware of the importance of the people retaining their primitive songs, has organised this competition to stimulate their performance, which in some areas are now almost completely forgotten.

The competition, subsidized by the Municipality with 12.000 pesetas, aims at the revival, maintenance and purification of the old *cante jondo* (also called sometimes *cante grande*). Today this not only lacks appreciation but is also considered an inferior kind of art, when on the contrary it is really one of the highest manifestations of folk art in Europe.

The competition will take place on the given dates and according to the following principles:

1. For the purposes of the competition, *cante jondo* will be considered to be the group of Andalusian songs, the generic type of which we believe to be the so-called *siguirilla gitana*. This is the origin of other songs still kept up by the people, like the *polos,* the *martinetes,* the *soleares,* which thanks to their very high qualities, distinguish themselves within the great group of songs commonly called *flamenco*. Strictly speaking, though, this last name should be applied only to the modern group formed by the *malagueñas,* the *granadinas* and their common stock, the *rondeñas*) to the *sevillanas,* the *peteneras,* etc., all of which can only be considered as derivatives of those we formerly named, and will therefore be excluded from the competition.

2. For qualification and award purposes, the songs will be grouped as follows:
   (a) *Siguirillas gitanas*
   (b) *Serranas*
   Polos
   Cañas
   Soleares

(c)   Songs without guitar accompaniment:
      Martinetes-Carceleras
      Tonás
      Livianas
      Saetas viejas

3.   All the *cantaores* of both sexes may take part in this competition. Only those professionals of less than twenty-one years will be allowed to participate. Professionals can send their students and in making awards the name of the master will be quoted.

4.   All those who give public performances who are engaged and paid by a theatrical company or by particular individuals will be considered as professionals.

5.   All those who want to register for the competition should fill in the attached form, and send it to the secretary of the Centro Artístico de Granada.

6.   The expiry date for registration is the 25th of May.

7.   To accompany the *cantaores* participating in the competition, guitar players will be admitted; they will be entitled to compete for the awards established for that purpose. Registration for guitar players is the same as for the *cantaores*; furthermore, their being professionals will be no obstacle to their registration.

8.   The competition will take place at the San Nicolás square (Albaicín) on the evenings of the 13th and 14th of June. The preliminary round will start on the 10th of June, at 10 o'clock, at the *Centro Artístico*. All the *cantaores* and *tocaores* must attend it; should they not do so, it will be understood that they no longer participate in the competition.

9.   The prizes will be distributed as follows:
      For the first group

Prize of Honour: 1.000 pesetas from the Municipality of Granada, and 1.000 pesetas from the special prize 'Ignacio Zuloaga'. In all, 2.000 pesetas.

First prize: 750 pesetas
Second prize: 500 pesetas
Third prize: 250 pesetas

For the second and third groups

Two first prizes of 1.000 pesetas each
Two second prizes of 500 pesetas each
Two third prizes of 250 pesetas each

For the guitar players

Special prize 'José Rodríguez Acosta': 1,000 pesatas
Second prize: 500 pesetas

10.   Competitors can participate in one or in several of the groups, but they can be awarded only one monetary prize. Should a competitor deserve several prizes, the highest of them will be handed to him, but of the others only an honourable qualification will be conferred on him. The amount outstanding on these prizes can be used to increase some of the others, should the jury judge it appropriate.

Rules for the Eliminating Rounds

These will be divided into two kinds of competitions:
1.   Admission tests
2.   Eliminating tests for the prizes.

The eliminating rounds will begin on 10th of June at 10 o'clock. All those who are registered must attend them; should they not do so it will be understood that they are no longer participating in the competition.

Admission tests. For those registered in the first group, this will consist of the performance of a *siguirilla gitana* of the simple sort (without the change). For those belonging to the second and to the third groups, it will consist of the performance of one of the songs in their group. As for the guitar players, it will consist of the accompaniment of the *cantaores* during the test.

Those of the *cantaores* and of the guitar players whose performances are to the satisfaction of the jury, will be entitled to participate in the *Eliminating test for the prizes.* These will be divided into three groups, corresponding to the three groups of the competition. The songs belonging to different groups will not be mixed.

In the first group, the competitor will sing two *siguirillas* of different styles, of his own choice.

In the second and third groups, it will be enough for the competitor to perform two songs belonging to two different items of the four comprised in either group.

Preference will be given to the performance of those songs which, because of their greater antiquity, are less known, since the main aim of the competition is to arouse interest in them.

Since only the performance of *siguirillas gitanas* is required for the first section, we should like to point out that in those of the *siguirillas* called *del cambio,* the *martinete* that sometimes accompanies them can also be sung.

Once the eliminating tests are completed, the jury will select from among the *cantaores* and the *tocaores* who have been examined, those who will take part in the competition and in the festival on the 13th and the 14th.

The verdict of the jury, as well as their decisions during the eliminating rounds, will be final.

The jury may interrupt the performance of the competitors whenever they think it convenient.

Remarks

We have to warn competitors most earnestly that preference will be given to those whose styles abide by the old practice of the classical *cantaores* and which avoids every kind of improper flourish, thus restoring the·*cante jondo* to its admirable sobriety, which was one of its beauties, and is now regrettably, lost.

For the same reasons, competitors should bear in mind that modernized songs will be rejected, however excellent the vocal qualities of the performer. Likewise, competitors should remember that it is an essential quality of the pure Andalusian *cante* to avoid every suggestion of a concert or theatrical style. The competitor is not a singer, but a *cantaor*.

The *cantaor* should not be discouraged if he is told that in certain notes he goes out of tune. On occasions, being out of tune is utterly irrelevant to the true connoisseur of Andalusian *cante*.

It should also be remembered that a great vocal range, that is, a voice that embraces many notes, is on the one hand necessary to the *cante jondo,* but on the other, its improper use can be detrimental to its stylistic purity.

NOTES

1. That rare treasure, the pure Andalusian song, not only threatens to disintegrate, but is on the verge of disappearing permanently. Something even worse is happening: with the exception of some *cantaor* still singing, and a few *ex cantaòres* with no voice left, what we can usually hear of the Andalusian song is a sad, lamentable shadow of what it was, of what it should be. The dignified, hieratic song of yesterday has degenerated into the ridiculous *flamenquism* of today. In this latter, the essential elements of Andalusian song, those which are its glory, its ancient nobility titles, are adulterated and (horror!) modernized. The sober vocal modulation – the natural inflexions of the song which cause the intervals between the notes of the scale to be divided and subdivided – has become an artificial ornamenting, more characteristic of the worst moments of the Italian decadent period than of the primitive songs of the East, with which ours can be compared

only when they are pure. The reduced melodic boundaries, within which our songs find their natural field, have been clumsily expanded. The modal wealth of the oldest scales has been replaced by the tonal poverty that the preponderant use of the only two modern scales causes, of those scales that monopolized European music during more than two centuries. Finally the phrase, crudely set in verse, is losing day by day the rhythmic flexibility that was one of its greatest beauties.

2. Juan Ruiz says:†

> Allí sale gritando la guitarra morisca,
> De las voces aguda, de los puntos arisca,
> El corpudo laúd, que tien' punto a la trisca,
> La guitarra latina con esto se aprisca.

That is:

> There the Moorish guitar starts shouting,
> with its sharp voice, with its harsh tones,
> the big-bodied lute also rejoices,
> the Latin guitar at that moment joins them.

and Pérez de Hita:

'He had a good voice; he played in Moorish as well as in the Castilian manner.'

Julio Cejador y Frauca, now considered the old-fashioned editor of the (alas!), only good annotated edition (there are many critical editions, but of no use to us) says that the Moorish guitar 'may be' the two-stringed instrument, very small and slender, the upper part of which, with no hole, is covered with parchment, found in Morocco and there called *quenbri;* whereas the guitar called *ladina* or *latina* is the Spanish guitar, of four orders of strings

---

† Juan Ruiz, also known as the Arcipreste de Hita, actually lived in the fourteenth century. His work is known as *Libro de Buen Amor* (Book of Good Love). (Trans.)